Relentless Hope

*Supernatural Christianity:
Establishing a New Normal*

Andy Merrick

Copyright © 2020 Andy Merrick

All rights reserved. This book is protected by the copyright laws of the United States of America. This book may not be copied or reprinted for commercial gain or profit. The use of short quotations or occasional page copying for personal or group study is permitted and encouraged. Permission will be granted upon request. Unless otherwise stated all Scripture quotations are from the ESV® Bible (The Holy Bible, English Standard Version®), copyright © 2001 by Crossway, a publishing ministry of Good News Publishers. Used by permission. All rights reserved. Scripture quotations marked (NIV) are taken from the Holy Bible, New International Version Anglicised Copyright © 1979, 1984, 2011 Biblica. Used by permission of Hodder & Stoughton Ltd, an Hachette UK company. Scripture quotations marked (AMP) are taken from the Amplified® Bible, Copyright © 2015 by The Lockman Foundation Used by permission. www.Lockman.org. Scripture quotations marked (MSG) are taken from THE MESSAGE, copyright © 1993, 2002, 2018 by Eugene H. Peterson. Used by permission of NavPress. All rights reserved. Represented by Tyndale House Publishers, Inc. All emphasis within Scripture quotations is the author's own. Please note that Destiny Image's publishing style capitalizes certain pronouns in Scripture that refer to the Father, Son, and Holy Spirit, and may differ from some publishers' styles.

DESTINY IMAGE® PUBLISHERS, INC.
P.O. Box 310, Shippensburg, PA 17257-0310
"Promoting Inspired Lives."

This book and all other Destiny Image and Destiny Image Fiction books are available at Christian bookstores and distributors worldwide.

Cover design by Esther Kotecha, EK Designs
Interior design by Avocet Typeset, Bideford, Devon, EX39 2BP

For more information on foreign distributors, call 717-532-3040.
Reach us on the Internet: www.destinyimage.com.

ISBN 13 TP: 978-0-7684-5726-1
ISBN 13 eBook: 978-0-7684-5727-8

Previously published under ISBN: 978-1-90815-445-3

For Worldwide Distribution.
1 2 3 4 5 6 7 8 / 24 23 22 21 20

TABLE OF CONTENTS

Praise for Relentless Hope — 5
Acknowledgements — 11
Foreword – Danny Silk — 13
Preface – Luke Merrick — 17

Introduction: Gideon's Story — 19
  The paper bag — 21
  Why this book? — 24

Part 1: Supernatural Culture — 27
  1.1 Is our culture killing us? — 27
  1.2 A revolution — 35
  1.3 Change the wineskin — 36
  1.4 Relational change — 39
  1.5 Coming out of hiding — 40
  1.6 Escape the malaise — 44
  1.7 Building good values — 51
  1.8 Miracles: our best argument — 53
  1.9 Honour the key to revival — 58
  1.10 Your worst nightmare — 61
  1.11 Love is Fierce — 63

Part 2: Only Human? — 71
  2.1 Finding myself in the kitchen — 71
  2.2 Who "I am" — 74
  2.3 He is in me — 77
  2.4 I am a grand design — 79
  2.5 In family Trinity — 84
  2.6 Sat in the right place — 87
  2.7 I can be who I was born to be — 89

Contents

2.8	The enemy's prime target revealed	92
2.9	Sons or servants?	96
2.10	Free from everything	98
2.11	Comfortable with the uncomfortable	101

Part 3: Intimacy and Encounter — 103

3.1	Struck dumb in prayer	104
3.2	Beholding	105
3.3	See God and die?	108
3.4	Stepping into encounter	110
3.5	More glory	117

Part 4: Is Heaven About to Collapse? — 121

4.1	A British problem?	121
4.2	Let's get all the verses together!	123
4.3	Jesus rewrote the rules	127
4.4	The only sensible conclusion	131
4.5	Is heaven about to fall?	132
4.6	New covenant	134
4.7	Sickness and suffering	136

Part 5: Why Apostles Are First? — 141

5.1	Transforming cities, transforming nations	141
5.2	Foundations	147
5.3	All about His presence	150
5.4	Apostolic teaching	153
5.5	The apostolic ministry of Jesus	158
5.6	Apostles, not teachers, first	161
5.7	Apostolic authority	163

Part 6: Hopes and Dreams — 167

6.1	Disappointment does not have to mean lost hope	167
6.2	Hope for good things	171
6.3	Bridging heaven and earth	173

Final word: Until — 179

PRAISE FOR RELENTLESS HOPE

I sat down to quickly skim Andy's book so I could write a short recommendation. Unfortunately, as soon as I started to read it I got hooked and found myself unable to put it down again! So, this recommendation took longer than I'd expected to write! But it was worth it because this is a terrific book – gripping, thought-provoking, challenging, honest and some of the paragraphs read like an edge-of-the-seat thriller! Not what I'd expected from "another Christian book" – it's fantastic!

There are some really good, life-changing teaching points on everything from the spiritual revival that's taking place globally to the importance of knowing who we are in God and being careful about what words we speak over ourselves. There is also a really useful chapter on the biblical role of apostles. Page after page is filled with some of the "hot" teaching topics the Holy Spirit is releasing to the church today, along with inspiring testimonies and keys for breakthrough. Andy has also included many personal insider views of some of the things he's struggled with over the years, which gives hope to the rest of us!

You can almost hear Andy's voice speaking the words as you read it – which is a good thing! Because Andy is a WYSIWYG kind of guy – "what you see is what you get" – thank God! So…don't just read this recommendation – buy a copy (in fact, buy several to give to other people too!). You will love it and it will change your life. Well done Andy!

Dr Barbara Jenkinson, Director, Light & Life International
Senior Leader, River Church

Relentless Hope

The ability and determination to keep on hoping is one of the most essential things in determining a fruitful life. This is true in all sectors of society, and for Christians hope forms part of the foundation upon which their faith can grow and flourish. "Faith is the assurance of things hoped for" (Hebrews 11:1).

Andy Merrick is a long-standing friend of mine; we have walked alongside each other in our pursuit of God, and have worked together to extend the Kingdom of Heaven and establish great churches. It is a deep friendship in which we have supported each other in the ups and downs of life, overcoming challenges and disappointments, and during this time I have seen Andy not only keep his hope alive but also allow his hope to flourish and grow with the outcome of greater fruitfulness in life.

In this book, *Relentless Hope*, Andy gives us insights into the things he has discovered whilst "en route with God." It is a book that contains wisdom from heaven, challenging thoughts, encouraging stories and great honesty with vulnerability.

God is definitely pouring out "new wine from heaven" at this moment in time, and the challenge is to create suitable new wineskins. I believe this book contains much helpful material that will give the reader an opportunity to reorder their thinking in order to keep pursuing God with relentless hope.

Amongst many things, personally I was stirred to think again about the verse, "Hope deferred makes the heart sick, but a longing fulfilled is a tree of life." Also, material on our union with Jesus, Healing, Apostles, and Hope stimulating God-given dreams make up the rich tapestry which this book weaves.

If you want to grow in your Christian faith, pursue a supernatural lifestyle and have a positive impact on the world around you, then *Relentless Hope* will help you on your journey.

PRAISE FOR RELENTLESS HOPE

"Love always protects, always trusts, always hopes, always perseveres. Love never fails." 1 Corinthians 13:7-8

Dr Pete Carter
Director of Eastgate
Founder of Heaven in Healthcare
Author of Unwrapping Lazarus

At a time when many are partnering with fear and scepticism, Andy Merrick refreshingly reminds us that the supernatural encompasses the Kingdom of Heaven. Part of activating the supernatural in our lives today lies in honouring the breakthrough of past revivalists.

In *Relentless Hope*, Andy uncovers the realities of our Western church culture and shows how our reluctance to honour the supernatural in our daily lives has kept us from experiencing all of God's promises for us today. But he doesn't stop there. Andy shares practical insights in how to grow in our identities in Christ and how we, as children of God, can use principles like honour, prayer and hope to steward and witness needed breakthrough in our lives.

Truly, *Relentless Hope* is a profound resource that will move you from the trappings of fear and propel you into new areas of miraculous encounters.

Dawna De Silva
Founder and co-leader of the international Sozo Ministry.
Co-author of Sozo: Saved, Healed, and Delivered,
Shifting Atmospheres, *and* Overcoming Fear.

Andrew and Theresa Merrick have been long-time friends to me and Katia. Few people I know have the authenticity, joy and most of all love that they carry. We have seen them become a significant force for the sake of the kingdom. After reading this book, I was reminded again of their journey of defeats and victories. It's this reality that qualifies them to talk about the amazing shift that God is bringing to the church. They have been forerunners in reforming the wineskin of their local church and as a result, impacted Glasgow and many other contexts in different nations.

What Andrew pens in this book are principles not just put together in the tower of theory but in the reality of practice. His insights into culture, the Kingdom of God, the supernatural and especially authentic apostles are profoundly theological and very highly reformational. For those who have been in church for a long time, it will bring a mind-shift and put adventure back into what it means to be a "normal" Christian. For those church leaders who are looking for "how to live out the kingdom," this book will give you handles on how to bring genuine transformation and not just behaviour modification. If you're a new Christian, this book will give you a glimpse into what following Jesus is really all about.

Katia and I cannot recommend this book highly enough. Many moments I was reminded of classic books I have read on revival, renewal and reformation, except with one significant difference: this book actually helps you journey into a lifestyle of apostolic Christianity as a usual way of living. It will stir your faith and build into you hope that will change your world!

Julian and Dr Katia Adams
Founders of Frequentsee, South Africa
Julian is the author of Gaining Heaven's Perspective and Kiss of the Father

PRAISE FOR RELENTLESS HOPE

So many books today talk about destination without helping us to understand the process of how to get there. *Relentless Hope* is a fresh, exciting book that charts a pastor's and his church's roadmap of moving from a hunger and desire to actually realising a supernatural Christianity and for it to become a culture within their church. This has not only changed their lives but is impacting the city of Glasgow and beyond with Kingdom breakthrough.

This book challenges much of our western methodology of "doing church" and trying to fulfil the great commission with a management/organisational structured approach. *Relentless Hope* highlights the need for an Apostolic mindset which is more akin to Saint Paul's missionary methods than what many experience today.

Jamie Watters
Senior Pastor
Glasgow Vineyard

Be inspired by Andy's passion for God's Kingdom to be displayed here and now on planet earth!

May *Relentless Hope* provoke an infectious confidence for you to rise up and play your part – "Christ in you the hope of Glory!"

Jeremy Simpkins
Leader, Christ Central Churches
(part of the Newfrontiers family)

ACKNOWLEDGEMENTS

Theresa, my lovely wife, thank you! Thanks for being a woman of undaunted faith, straightforward integrity and genuine love. Everything in this book, though written by my hand, belongs to you just as much.

Thanks to my children and their partners. Most of them have contributed by reading, commenting, editing and encouraging the production of this book and all of them have lived through some of the challenges of getting here. So Dan and Anny, Jess and Andi, Luke and Claire and Kez and Joe, heartfelt appreciation.

Thanks to those who the helped editorially and have given hours to make this look decent and make sense – Jan McFarlane, Fiona Urqhart and Ian Hawkins, you made it possible.

Finally, I can only say thank you to Hope Church and its courageous leaders who have lived the ups and downs of this journey and still do. You worship with whole hearts and have great courage to embrace the new and at times experimental. You have listened well as I've tried to explain what at times is unexplainable, but it means we have the chance to live in something wonderful. Thanks for keeping saying yes to the Holy Spirit.

FOREWORD

Hope sets us up to be looking for something or someone good. Growing up in a rural northern California mountain town, it was not unusual for someone to get lost in the woods. Sometimes it was a small child or an elderly person who'd wandered too far from home. Other times it was someone who'd been out there before hunting or hiking, but somehow lost their way. Whoever it was or why they were lost, they had to find themselves in a mental space where they turned to hope. They needed to have hope that someone was looking for them. They needed to believe that they would be found.

I see the New Covenant as this type of hope. As soon as one of us realizes that we are lost, we begin to look for the hope of being found. We need to believe that someone knows where we are and how to get to us. We need them to have hope as well. Not only while they are searching with all their available resources, but in their relentless pursuit to find us.

When we see Jesus looking through the crucifixion and seeing joy, we know that He is fuelled by wild, passionate hope. He is hoping that His Father is powerful and capable. His joy rests in the character of His Father and the wholeness they will achieve together creating a "new covenant" with mankind. Jesus has this unflinching hope that He is doing what He needs to do and that His Father is coming to get him. They are two powerful people working together to accomplish a world-changing goal. Jesus and His father have an honouring, loving connection.

To understand this honour, we need to understand what it

means to live a powerful life. Power is essential to freedom. Our lives are designed to produce freedom within the context of love. Love introduces a choice. Choice introduces options besides love. We must realize that Jesus looked at that cross and had other options than to do it. He had other options than joy. No one could make Jesus go through what he chose to do for us all. Therefore, if we are to have free, loving relationships we must know what to do with power. Being a powerful person is what it takes to represent our Father accurately on this earth.

No one feels honoured by someone who is powerless. God is not looking for slaves to bow down to Him, to boss around or to rule over. He is looking for people who will love and honour Him. He is looking for people whom He can love and honour. Powerless people are consumers in relationships. They are anxious about their survival and absorbed with themselves. Love does not live in relationships where there is no power, where there is a lack of honour. Love requires us to be powerful, responsible decision-makers. It is powerful people who build powerful, loving, lasting families.

God is love. He is the foundation of what love behaves like. The Bible is not a historical snapshot of God. It is the history of man in his relationship with love. Why would God introduce a poor choice in a perfect garden scene in the beginning of mankind's story? If He was going for control, He could have secured it right there in the beginning. But instead, a loving Father introduced the ingredient that insures freedom, a choice. The choice that demonstrated that our God was looking for a love relationship with the mankind He had created. This messy story all begins with mankind learning to be a powerful, responsible lover.

I often wonder what our world would've looked like if Adam, when confronted by God about the decision to partake of the forbidden fruit, had asked for forgiveness. We know that

Foreword

his response was to shift blame and avoid responsibility. He says, "That woman that You gave me ..." and the rest is history. Adam avoids the responsibility that his freedom requires and love suffers the most. But God knows how to be a loving parent even better than we do. He will not give up on mankind no matter how selfish, destructive and irresponsible he decides to become.

Each party has a choice about what they will bring to the relationship. God is consistently faithful, gracious and forgiving. The Bible is a record of this. Those who seek to find Him find that He wants us all to know this about Him. He wants us to know Him as a lover who empowers us to be free so that we can in return offer the same to Him. So many of us who believe never learn that we are powerful to bring the offering of love, honour and connection. Mysteriously, we get snagged in the realm of obediently approaching a stoic father who angers easily and is, in general, unpleasant. Nothing could be farther from the truth!

What reward could there be for God to create us and then hide Himself from us? What reward does a father have in abandoning his children? There isn't one. He's not insecure, nor is He irresponsible, therefore the perception issue must be on our end. God wants the world of His creation to be reconciled to Him through the work we now know as the New Covenant.

Andy is going to lead us through this process of understanding who our Father is and to what lengths He will go to accomplish this great reconciliation. This book, *Relentless Hope,* is a survey of this process and a road map to reconnect to our Father's heart. God wants our help to reconcile the world to Himself through his Body. Jesus teaches the disciples to pray "Your Kingdom come, Your will be done on earth as it is in Heaven." Andy will show us how the Gifts of Christ are essential for us to begin constructing the vehicle of bringing Heaven to earth. Heaven flowing to earth is dependent on the Church rediscovering how our present government competes with what God has ordered in His Church. The order of the priorities on earth must change to match what a loving Father needs for His Kingdom to flourish around us.

Understanding the role of apostles is crucial to a healthy and effective Church on the earth. Andy has a great grasp on the function of the apostle and the priority of the presence of God taking a rightful place in how we operate in church leadership. Unlocking the apostolic and prophetic applications to our daily lives and church government are keys to realizing the Kingdom of God on the earth.

It is a great pleasure for me to recommend *Relentless Hope* to you as you pursue what it means to live in the freedom God entrusts you with. My prayer when all is said and done is for love to be the greatest signature on this generation. God bless you!

Danny Silk
President of Loving on Purpose
Danny serves on the Senior Leadership teams of both Bethel Church in Redding, California and Jesus Culture in Sacramento, California

PREFACE

Growing up as a pastor's kid is a bit of a mixed bag: life is full of the iconic leftover meeting food that's made up of that unique combination of cakes, biscuits and quiche; there are loud early-morning prayer meetings that wake you up with off-key singing more often than you'd like; and there's a never-ending supply of misfits, outcasts and weirdos whom you're told to be nice to because Jesus loves them.

One of the big positives for me was that I got to witness my dad's radical and faithful pursuit of God's seemingly-unattainable promises over many years first-hand. There's something powerful in watching someone go through incredible difficulty and opposition and not give up. Even more so when what happens on the other side of that season is miraculous.

In many ways, this book is about my dad's life; a life defined by the same kind of radical, restless and relentless hope that you find in the stories of Abraham, David, Paul and countless others. This is the sort of biblical hope that we all need in order to see the fullness of Christ's awesomeness on Earth today.

So make yourself a cup of tea, find a comfy chair, and prepare to have your socks blown off, your faith stretched and your hope galvanised.

Luke Merrick

INTRODUCTION

Gideon shared his story

"One day we had a lady who was admitted with shortness of breath due to a chest infection." Gideon, who is part of our church and works as a support worker on a respiratory ward, was calmly telling me his latest story. "She had a history of conditions that had blocked and scarred the airways in her lungs (COPD and bronchiectasis). She had been given proper medications and continuous care from the medical doctors, nurses and physios and was given humidified oxygen. Despite all of this her condition didn't seem to get any better; in fact, after a few weeks she became confused, her mobility reduced significantly and her exercise tolerance became poor. I gave her numerous physio and OT sessions and I didn't see any improvement. Eventually she was moved to an isolation room as she contracted MRSA – that's a superbug resistant to antibiotics.

"Six weeks passed and our lovely patient's condition kept deteriorating. Her room had all the tubes and machines you can imagine and she had no appetite, she lost weight, she complained of pain due to a severe collection of fluid in her body (a condition called oedema.)

"I regularly pray in the ward, but having a patient for six weeks and not seeing any improvement started to make me feel hopeless; my prayers seemed to not be working. One Friday afternoon I went to see this patient, and she declined our session. She was very emotional that day and was telling me that she missed her family so much, that she just wanted to go home, but in her situation that seemed impossible. She told me that the only thing that could bring her home was a MIRACLE. Then she told me that she didn't believe in miracles. So I quickly replied to her that 'I do believe in miracles.' Then I asked her if I could pray for her, and she said yes. I laid my hand on her legs and said a simple prayer for healing. After praying I looked her in the eye, took a risk and declared to her, 'You are going home this weekend to be with your family.'

"I went in on the Monday and found she was still there, but the staff nurse told me that she was ready for discharge. She had improved over the weekend, and had not been discharged because she needed to see a physio first. The oedema had gone, she tested negative for MRSA, and she was off the oxygen and the IV drip. The physiotherapist was still concerned about whether she could walk unaided, so we took in a walking frame. As we entered her room she was happily and loudly telling the physiotherapist, 'He prayed for me, he prayed for me (she was pointing at me), I am well now.' Then she was begging the physio to let her go home. And then she stood up, walked independently out of her room to the stairs outside the ward, and climbed a flight of stairs. She went home that day!"

God is moving around the world in unprecedented ways. It used to be that we would hear great miracle stories from Africa, but now they are happening on the streets and in the hospitals of my city and that experience is being replicated around the western world, which hitherto seemed insulated from these sorts of supernatural experiences. Something is changing.

Although I'd dreamed for decades of church life filled with the supernatural, of Christians displaying the full nature of Jesus, not just great character, I was a bit shut down. Real hope of such a dream was flickering at best, and you will read of some of my struggles through this book. I didn't really have eyes to see clearly what He had begun to do. And then we went through a significant trauma, and God woke us up.

The Paper Bag

We should have been dead.

As a church we should not have survived. So many bad things hit the fan inside one year, we were in a real mess. As a leader I was advised to move away and give up on the dream I had. On the inside I was done, drained, depressed; to quote Theresa (my wife), "You looked like an empty paper bag, a shadow of what you were." I was like a Happy Meal with no "happy"; the carton but no toy. So many things had gone wrong it must be my fault, that's what people said, and I was hurting. "No smoke without fire" was the motto. And it wasn't just me, many of us were toast; burned on both sides and not much oomph for church or faith for much. In fact, we had attracted a few people who had already been burned by church and now this one seemed to be on fire.

We had faced some extreme hidden sin; how could it live in church and we not know? We faced baseless accusations; how could such dishonour thrive amongst God's people? We experienced relational tension and breakdown; how could that be in a relational movement? We believed in miracles and were seeing what appeared to be defeat and enemy activity for which we had no answer. Hope's flames were extinguished by a year of unfortunate events, or poor decisions, depending on your point of view! We'd had a passion for the glorious church, a church to change a city and a nation. Now we were just thinking about surviving. We were in deep disappointment and hope was in short supply.

Many of us were desperate; we were open to reviewing how we came to such a place. For me, I felt the many years of ministry I had under my belt had not adequately prepared me for this. The experience opened many of us up to new thinking. I had real questions about how I had built, who I was and what I was called to do. I had twenty-plus years' ministry experience at this point and I was hungry for change.

Seeds of Hope

We clung together (thank God for an amazing wife and friends who stood close), God kept showing up, and some prophets prophesied such outrageous things over us that we were unable to believe them at the time. The likelihood of such wonders happening with us looked slim to none. But we tentatively began a new journey, resurrection happened, hope sprang up.

We discovered there is *no reason on this earth* to abandon hope.

We started to see how we saw ourselves; we thought we were pretty powerless, and had become victims as a result. It was like looking in a mirror – staring back at us was what we really believed about our identity, and it was flawed, not what Jesus paid for.

We began to understand that we had a culture, what that was, and that it had many dysfunctional aspects. So we set about reforming it. We didn't have a grid for culture, though, and it took a while.

We began to see that although we said we had a value for His presence and miracles, we didn't value them in the true sense. We had fear and questions deeper than faith. We had a theology based on experience rather than truth.

We began to see miracle after miracle; deafness healed, creative miracles, some incurable diseases healed, people having wonderful God encounters, angels showing up in worship, massive angels showing up in prayer meetings, and people having trances. These things raised questions of their own, but hope was also rising!

What we found out was that God is moving powerfully across the globe; that power from on high is being poured out and that the 21st century Church is being invited into a cultural transformation rarely seen in church history. The Spirit is saying something to the Church, and as she is listening, remarkable things are happening around the planet. It took several crises to make us listen and to help us see the awesomeness of what God is about.

In a revolution

We are in the midst of a Holy Spirit revolution, a reformation of thought and culture, a revolution characterised by a total focus on the manifest presence of God flowing into miracles and healings, a reformation in believers' sense of identity, an overwhelming revelation of the Father's love, and a fresh understanding of apostolic ministry.

All that was happening inspired a fresh digging into scripture. We wanted to be diligent and scriptural, especially as some of the things we were seeing and ideas we were having were off our normal charts.

God used the nightmare to wake us up, to help us reconsider our ways and to plug us deeper into what He was doing around the world. We got our hope back. We got a window into the majestic purposes of God being unfolded in our time.

Many people are aware that things are shifting and changing. You don't have to go through a trauma to wake up, to question. God is wakening His people up to new thinking and possibilities. There is hunger for more everywhere. People are asking questions about the church and faith and hope. They are aware the old paradigms and cultures need examining. To some it's confusing, to some it's exciting and to some it's both. To some it feels painful and to some it's joyful, and you guessed it, others feel both. We have experienced all these emotions.

Why This Book?

I am seeking to inspire radical, restless and relentless hope in you, the sort of biblical hope that we all need in order to see the fullness of Christ's awesomeness on Earth today. The sort of hope that means you don't give up; the sort of hope that means you will see the goodness of God manifest in and through you. Hope that will propel and sustain your journey into the Jesus normal of supernatural Christianity.

The journey raises questions, which this book also seeks to answer in order to remove roadblocks from our hearts and minds, and to help us see with greater clarity and so move with greater confidence. The key questions we will look at as we journey through the different sections of this book are:

1) The supernatural makes me uncomfortable; how can I embrace God's power and not hold back?
2) How do I become more effective in displaying His supernatural power and love?
3) Are these invasions of God occasional or normal?
4) What's God's opinion of me and is it important I agree?
5) What's God's will regarding healing? The Bible seems contradictory on this point, and my experiences are patchy.
6) Why are apostles vital to what God is doing?
7) How can I keep hope alive when I experience disappointments?

Think of each section and chapter as a building block, each

Introduction

one essential to build the completed structure. Together they give a fuller answer to the questions posed above. Or think of them as colours that paint a picture to inspire, to shed light and to move fears and misconceptions aside.

May this book be a window for you; may you see more of heaven, more of God. Let it be a point of illumination and inspiration; may it be a source of relentless hope to you!

PART 1

SUPERNATURAL CULTURE

It was news to many of us that we had a culture. We just lived inside a set of standard Christian beliefs that were commonly accepted. It was even bigger news to realise it was crucial to what we were or weren't experiencing from heaven and how comfortable we might be with that!

1.1 Is Our Culture Killing Us?

What is culture? Is it going to ballet or listening to classical music? Well, those are cultural activities. But what we are setting out to discuss here is more the thinking and beliefs that govern behaviour and habits in any given nation or people group. There's a two-way street between cultural expressions like the arts and cultural beliefs themselves. Artistic expressions can inspire and accelerate cultural change, but they also express the spirit of the age from which they are emerging.

Culture is expressed in things like Bonfire Night in the UK...why do we do that again? It was the Gunpowder Plot. On 5th November 1605, Guy Fawkes, a member of the Gunpowder Plot, was arrested as he guarded a large amount of gunpowder under the House of Lords. The plot, to blow up Parliament and with it King James the First (of England; he was James the Sixth of Scotland), was foiled and bonfires were lit in celebration. Now, over 400 years later, it's a cultural event where every year we get to make big fires and let off lots of fireworks...and sometimes burn effigies of Guy Fawkes! Much of the original purpose has been forgotten but we all do make fires and explosions on a dark November night every year.

In the US, huge firework displays accompany Fourth of July Independence Day celebrations, celebrating the declaration of independence from the British – the people who burn Guy Fawkes effigies. On July 4th and November 5th, lots of fireworks burn bright for very different historic and cultural reasons. In one case the reasons and feelings behind it are clear; in the other they are a bit lost in the mists of time, but we Brits still religiously cling to the celebration of Bonfire Night. In one case the celebration re-enforces a key cultural value and celebrates a defining moment in history; in the other the habit is entrenched but the reasons are foggy. The Brits are no longer celebrating the defence of Parliament, they are just having fun!

A good while ago, as a management studies undergraduate, I came across Peter Drucker. He was seen as one of the major management gurus of the 20th century. One of his famous sayings was "culture eats strategy for breakfast." What he meant was, you can come up with all the best strategies to make changes in an organisation and bring progress, but the pervading culture is the thing which decides whether they will succeed or not. For example, if you have a culture of disloyalty in your organisation, where managers have been careless in the way they looked after employees, there will be little compunction from employees to loyally support new strategies that inconvenience them in any way. A genius strategy that requires inconveniencing a resentful workforce will struggle for any kind of traction.

We were taught in some mind-stretching lectures that

company directors and CEOs had the job of producing culture in their businesses. It was a bigger remit than I had imagined. I thought naively that it was just about running a company to "make widgets for a profit." What we saw was that business leaders, whether consciously or otherwise, create an environment in which the widgets are made and the profit is measured. They get to say things like: "We will be profitable regardless of how poorly we treat our employees" or: "In this company we will make our product and we will be honest, even if it costs us; we will strive for worker satisfaction because we believe happy workers make more excellent things." These are all "philosophy of business" statements which, when backed by appropriate actions, will create very different company atmospheres.

Christians and churches have their own cultures. These cultures can facilitate our strategies or frustrate them. For instance, we may have a winning evangelistic strategy, but no one outside of church wants to come close because of our reputation for judgment. Often there is great clarity behind things we do in church; in other areas we know our behaviours are important but struggle to remember why. Culture that was developed to preserve, promote and protect key values in a church or denomination can become a hindrance. Being organisationally self-aware of what we are breeding in our atmosphere is really vital.

I am aware of a nation where there's a large denomination whose culture is extremely democratic and committee-driven to the point that it's very difficult for leaders to lead at all. Leaders have no greater influence than any other voice on the board or committee. It was set up this way to preserve the truths that ignited its existence. These were truths precious to its founders and, as that fuelled its success, no one should have the power to change them. Now it's one of the fastest declining groups on the planet because the culture strongly resists change. All the wonderful structures and habits, beliefs and practices are inhibiting new strategies to bring much-needed change and growth. The energies and creativity of its leaders are drained away in the struggle against the prevailing culture.

<u>Changing our Nations?</u>

Those of us who live in the western world are generally surrounded by a mindset that doesn't expect the supernatural. This is all-pervading and treats supernatural claims with great suspicion and caution; or, bizarrely, as something fun and harmless. So people host mediums in their home and run it like a Tupperware party!

As believers we are perhaps right to ask ourselves whether we should expect cultural transformation and reformation in such a secular environment. Can sophisticated nations and cities be changed through a move of Holy Spirit like we see in the book of Acts and in church history? In our history we have great examples; William Wilberforce, the great reformer who got slavery abolished in early 19th century Britain, was part of the Clapham sect of Christian leaders who had the mission "to make goodness fashionable." They had far-reaching influence that led to some declaring that the ethos of the Clapham sect became the spirit of the age in Victorian Britain. Can this happen again? If so, how?

The culture we are surrounded by poses all kinds of challenges to the church and the gospel and many are working hard at solutions.

Is our cultural relevance – our ability to connect to it and affect it – found in tracking its trends and trying to plug our Gospel into them? How are we to maintain relevance? We have many 'seeker-sensitive' models trying to solve these riddles and appeal to mainstream western culture.

The Church's mission, however, is cultural transformation.

Jesus called us to disciple nations. This surely involves influence across every level of a nation's structures, beliefs and behaviours. The Clapham sect understood this. They shaped culture, rather than being shaped by it.

To be effective in nation-changing we need to understand and renew our own cultural models, taking time to figure out if we are exporting what we really value. In our journey we found our beliefs and aspirations were not matched by the fruit we were bearing. For instance, we found sin was being hidden, relationships were not robust and people struggled to hold onto one another if the going got really tough. But we believed in relationships. Our outreach was recruitment-based and as a result people could smell that agenda coming at them from a mile away; but we thought and believed in unconditional love. We asked the question: would the world around us want our influence when we appeared in reality to struggle with the same things as they did in their relationships and motives?

Do we need more mission, more evangelism, more church planting? Will filling the nation with more churches automatically achieve culture transformation? I used to think it would, but the light began to dawn that the kind of churches we were creating was probably more important than how many we had or even how big they were.

Are our seeker-friendly services, our mission activity and our church plants reproducing a culture that is transforming the world or reflecting it? Are we copying years of established Christian values and just repackaging them with no analysis of our approach or assessment of the real fruit they bear? On Bonfire Night we always light fires, but our reasons for doing so are now a little hazy. Have we understood that evangelical and charismatic Christianity has a culture that we export and express in everything we do? Is that culture one that Jesus generated around him? We know He struggled to keep crowds away and He had no social media; in fact He had no kind of media at all.

Have we understood what we project as Christian culture to the world? Church-planting and mission can simply be ways of packaging and exporting a culture we are unaware of and that culture is in many cases eating our strategies for breakfast. What kind of churches are we planting, what is the content of our message, and more importantly, what attitudes and beliefs are we communicating in our chosen methodologies and words? What kind of atmosphere do people encounter when they come in contact with our communities?

Danny Silk said to us once, "You don't export your message, you don't export your ministry, you export your culture."

Assessing these issues requires self-awareness, which is why often it's only in a crisis that we become willing to look at our fundamental assumptions and modes of operation. Assessment also requires courage. Christians invest heavily in what they believe; time, money, emotion, prayer and energy are poured into vision carried by ministries and churches. Churches and movements need these things feeding their momentum to be sustained and to succeed. Reviewing the basic tenets or ways of working can be very scary because of the investment by many in the status quo.

If we stopped Bonfire Night because no one knew why we did it anymore, wouldn't that put firework companies out of business? Any change can create misunderstanding; any review can imply a lack of commitment to the cause. Review is fraught with challenges. We need courage to face the real answers about what our lives, churches and movements model to the world around us. We need courage to face the answers when we don't like them! Courage to inspect the fruit at a more than superficial quantity-based assessment.

Our Father is a master fruit inspector; we can partner with His expert eye rather than resist His discipline (John 15).

We became aware, at various points, that our culture was frustrating our desires. Our aspirations were great, and we thought we had and understood love and faith; but our fruit was a bit mottled. We saw how our love could so easily be eaten by judgement, transparency be hindered by the presence of fear, and supernatural breakthrough blocked by scepticism and reserve.

<u>Jesus the one-man culture creator</u>

Jesus was heaven manifest on the earth. He brought the flavour, the very atmosphere He lived in for eternity, to the earth. Supernatural events, miracles, love, freedom, and wisdom oozed out of him. There was so much heavenly juice pouring out of Jesus that thousands of men, women and children could sit for days (e.g. feeding the 4,000) and listen despite having no food or multimedia presentation to keep them engaged (though I am not against such technology or using such tools!).

He was surprising and unconventional. He wasn't unconventional because He had examined and rejected the conventions around him, decided they weren't for Him and so created a counterculture to expose the failings of the system He saw. He wasn't a reaction. Earth was reacting to Him. He was bringing to bear the feelings, the values, the atmosphere He enjoyed with Father and Holy Spirit. Heaven has a culture and He personified it on earth. There were no guilt trips, shame or religious pressure coming from Him. He was 100% real, no tricks, nothing fake, no performing to make up for a lack of charisma. He just released freedom to those around Him; freedom from sickness, satanic oppression, religious burdens and unhealthy belief systems.

Wrapped up in all this was an invitation to follow, to become friends, to become disciples, to take up His yoke. In following you became authorised to do the same things He did. You were taught to pray that God's will, which in Jesus' hands looked pretty wonderful, would be done on earth "as it is in heaven." Presumably He was thinking "as it is in heaven" means with the same style, grace and flavour as heaven's Father-Son-and-Spirit celestial society, God's will done His way, not just any old way. His highest value was not compliance, or God's will no matter what; but God's will in His style. Jesus was exporting a whole culture, a feel, a style, an atmosphere – not a set of activities and words. He came to bring heaven to earth.

No wonder "supernatural" is rising in the Christian vocabulary and "heaven invading earth" is being spoken about around the world. Heaven's style is supernatural style, unlimited by earth's normal boundaries. No wonder we became challenged in the way we interpreted love and honour. The Trinity's intimacy looked a lot different to our relational dynamics.

In summary

Healthy culture helps momentum increase. Healthy culture is attractive in and of itself and is therefore transformational. Whether we are aware of it or not, like it or not, we export our culture. Our attitudes, beliefs and behaviours shout much louder than our message or ministry.

Initiatives and strategies that fail because of cultural weaknesses are very disappointing. Unhealthy culture eats our world-transforming strategies.

Healthy culture provides a great environment for the supernatural to continually manifest.

1.2 A revolution

A story appeared in a Scottish daily newspaper. The police were telling the story of a house they were called out to. The residents were experiencing strange phenomena and were very scared and were being advised to move out. The police described light fittings that were moving on their own, clothes being strewn around, and one officer observed a dog in the garden that was at one moment on the lawn and in the next on top of a six foot (1.8m) hedge. They had no explanation, and no crime had been committed but the householders were scared.

Jen, one of our leaders, received a phone call from a Christian friend. He happened to be connected to the family in this house. He phoned Jen and said words to the effect, "You know about this kind of spiritual stuff. Can you help?" That was really the wrong question to ask Jen. If you know her you know she is totally up for this kind of thing and these sorts of opportunities get her excited. So a visit was arranged, and to cut a long story short, Jen discerned the spirit that was functioning this way and kicked it out in Jesus' name and the hassle stopped. When it started again she revisited and found the family had unwittingly re-invited the unwanted guest. Jen removed the offending spirit again, gave instruction on what to do, and one of the women in the house got healed of arthritis. All the nonsense stopped. Who you gonna call!?

All kinds of supernatural stuff is happening. Some Christians are claiming angelic visitation, transcendent encounters, experiences of bi-locating, visionary experiences, many dramatic healings and creative miracles. We have to learn how to engage in this fresh emphasis on the supernatural. These experiences produce hope and excitement in believers and also call us to explore biblical foundations and to get ready for the powerful things God wants to do in and through us.

Jesus is committed to the commission He gave us – heal the sick, raise the dead, cleanse lepers, cast out demons. You received without paying; give without pay (Matthew 10:8). He doesn't have a new commission or a different idea. And we don't need a new one because this remains powerful and effective in any culture in any generation. When is it not relevant to heal the sick? He is committed to drawing us back to the authentic expression of the original blueprint He gave over two thousand years ago.

This is a revolution where we have experienced cripples dancing on our streets and destinies being called out of weary unbelievers. Believers are imparting the tangible presence of God to those around them, and they get a reputation in their gyms and workplaces for being those with 'healing hands'. It's a revolution where everything we do as churches gets to be charged with the supernatural presence of God, where our mercy ministries are characterised by bringing people into experiences of God, not just giving them food – as good as that is.

1.3 Change the Wineskin

It's impossible for God to move and our "Christian culture" not be challenged and changed. New wine is by nature active and fizzy; it needs a supple container, not something stiff and old. The scripture tells us that the vibrancy of the new wine can actually destroy an old wineskin if it's used.

The most vivid biblical example of this would be the outpouring of the Spirit in Acts 2. It required a whole new structure and set of values. The early disciples devoted themselves to the apostles' teaching, not the rabbis'. They met in houses, and evangelists and prophets emerged who were not regulated by the Sanhedrin; and it became apparent that the Jewish legalistic faith was being challenged by grace–grace that required faith and not ceremony.

When the Charismatic renewal of the 1960s and 1970s hit the church it brought not just tongues and prophecy, but a change in church culture. Worship changed, the way it did community changed, house groups became common, and fresh theologies took root, such as the 'already and not yet' view of the kingdom – a view that said the kingdom of God was available now as well as after Jesus' return. The constant use of charismatic gifts and regular experiences of the Spirit challenged structures and expectations and asked fresh questions of leadership. The transition now from Charismatic to "consistently supernatural" is another sea-change, another culture shift. This shift means having churches moving continually in signs and wonders and comfortable with heavenly realities invading; churches where dreams and visions are normal and are given real significance. This is a big shift, and we should expect that much cultural transformation is necessary to cooperate with such change.

Our inherited church culture, if we are honest, has grown up around a limited amount of supernatural activity, and probably a large amount of disappointment and some judgement. Also, our society's culture has to some degree bled into the church. In the UK we can be quite cynical, lacking hope. We value self-deprecation, tend to criticise and be suspicious of the successful (something called the "tall poppy syndrome"). We are a pluralistic and postmodern society. This means we are supposed to respect what everyone thinks but please don't get too excited about your thing, because no one thing is better or more truthful than another.

For the supernatural to become normal in our experience

and take root in the culture of our churches, we have to remove the negative approaches that stifle its spread and deaden our responses. God looks to us to actively steward what He deposits (see the parable of the talents, for example), not just observe and analyse. A culture of low expectation inherited from our past, and the cautious reception of the invasion of the realms of heaven inherited from the prevailing mood, quickly suck the life out of God-initiated breakthroughs and miracles. When this happens it's hard to maintain traction and gain momentum. We need to replace our "analyse and observe" culture with a culture that fans the flames and stokes the fire. Analysis and observation have value, but on their own breed detachment rather than engagement. We can end up with God as entertainer, a God whom we test and judge rather than a Father whom we embrace and who gives gifts we treasure.

In all that He is doing, Heavenly Father is moving us away from anything earth-based to reflect the culture that exists around Him, so that our communities taste and feel more authentically filled with His values and His life.

He is calling for us to learn not to quench or grieve the Holy Spirit by our attitudes, behaviours or structures, and create wineskins that can hold the new wine of Heaven. He is asking us to be actively engaged in what it takes to fan into flame the gifts given to us corporately and individually. We have a responsibility to partner with the work of the Holy Spirit. He may move sovereignly but we cooperate intentionally and hopefully willingly. The outcome is then meant to be MORE FIRE. Our active partnership with the Holy Spirit is meant to increase what He is doing, to magnify it, to fan His flame so it burns brighter (1 Thessalonians 5:19; Ephesians 4:30; 2 Timothy 1:6).

1.4 Relational Change

We behave out of what we believe and the outcome is culture. As expressed above, culture is a set of beliefs through which we do life and view life, and these beliefs produce a set of behaviours and routines. Culture creates an atmosphere, a feeling, that those around and among us can detect. It can be cold, welcoming, fun, serious, exciting, accepting, friendly or judgemental. People don't have to be born again to detect an agenda, a negative atmosphere or mood in a house, a community, or even a city.

Our culture is the sum of our behaviours toward people, both in and outside the church. As we have seen above, it's about how we work with supernatural presence, but it's also about how we respond to people. We can test how well we are receiving the Lord by how we receive one another, how well we love the Lord by our love for one another. Environments where criticism flows easily and judgement comes up in our hearts toward others are not reflecting the reality that mercy triumphs over judgement. Heavenly Father constantly treats us better than we deserve. Reflecting that strongly in our church families would change us (1 John 4:20 and Matthew 20, where the workers in the vineyard get equal pay for shorter hours... outrageously amazing).

We found in this move of God that He is addressing how we treat one another. His presence both produces unity and calls for increased heart connection. His manifest presence puts a new demand on our relationships and togetherness. He is lifting up the importance of covenant in relationship, vulnerability and honour.

He is teaching the church to love, unpacking what He means by that; making us aware of His standard and His empowerment in the realm of relating to other human beings. It appears that love has been hijacked and redefined and then re-installed in the church as something less than the original. What we thought was love was too tame. It wasn't fierce enough. What we thought were relationships weren't deep enough in the commitment sense. There was way too much fear lurking in our environment for authentic love to flourish well. Fear of what people think, of what might happen, of how I look, is the fear of man and it snares us every time we live from it.

So much disappointment in church life is rooted in relational problems. Authentic love and honour help us stay healthily connected and so keep hope flourishing (see 1.9 – Honour, the key to Revival).

1.5 Coming Out of Hiding

For a long time I languished in disappointment in the area of healing. In an exciting season in my life I had seen some great healings and done regular healing meetings. It had been a scary ride, standing in the front of a meeting saying God that heals today and then stepping out believing something would happen now. The first time was the toughest! It did make us cry out to God, though, and we saw some amazing breakthroughs. But my faith and enthusiasm were punctured as we buried a cancer patient. She was a beautiful two-year-old girl with a large tumour on the side of her neck. Her non-Christian parents had brought her to us. We were their last hope. They had heard about our meetings and our offer of healing. The toddler died and disappointment seeped into my soul. Another cancer patient that we prayed for died, and then a while later my friend's teenage son died of a brain tumour. Some deep negativity took root.

In this season a young woman lodged with us who had severe joint pain all over her body. She had a tough and abused background and already arthritis was working in her body. After work she couldn't even climb the stairs to her bedroom. She was in so much pain and exhaustion she had to lie on a sofa for half an hour to get the strength to climb one flight of stairs. She wore splints on her wrists for support and tried to manage her condition as best she could. She was only in her early twenties and this much pain so early in life was not good news. She asked for prayer and I agreed to it, then forgot; in reality, I put it off as I had such low expectations. Eventually I prayed with her. It was an extremely low-key event; I felt nothing and neither did she. About a week later I heard her bouncing a basketball in our yard and thought it was strange as it would hurt her wrists. Our whole family started to notice changes in her behaviour. She started to come home looking a bit sweaty. So after about a week of this we asked how she was doing. She said she had no pain and had been checking out her joints, running home from work, bouncing basketballs. She joined the soccer team and played badminton and eventually got into some extreme sports. She was healed, completely healed!

Around that time I was leading a "Churches Together" group in our city and we called some joint prayer meetings where Christians from all backgrounds came together. During one of these meetings, the presence of God was intense and I decided to call people forward for prayer, including for healing. Two of our young guys prayed for a certified blind man. He had the cane, the guide dog, the dark glasses and received the disability benefit to go with it. They prayed and he got healed, his sight returned and he gave his dog back!

It seems strange now, but none of these breakthroughs pushed me out of my funk. My default posture was to remain disappointed and cautious, whilst still believing and having a go at healing sometimes. I was in a place of unresolved tension on these issues.

On reflection the environment these miracles happened in was strange too. Even among the Charismatic fraternity there seemed to be caution and even a little cynicism about these breakthroughs. They weren't heralded or celebrated as I thought they would be among those of us who believed for such things. We had medical evidence for the blind man who was healed. We were all praying for amazing things but when they came we were a bit aloof from them. These brief seasons of miracles would quickly fade and be forgotten.

A tactic I adopted to try and reconcile my belief with my lack of consistent results and low motivation was to invite people who were more effective. In Newcastle-upon-Tyne, where we were based at that time, we invited an evangelist who was seeing some healing and we saw results particularly in the realm of hearing loss. But when he left the momentum left with him. Later we moved to plant a church in Glasgow and I got to know an American who was up for praying for the sick and saw some results, so I asked him to pray for some people. In reality I was hiding behind these people; disappointment was still ruling and providing a place for fear in my heart. I didn't want to be the one taking the risk of disappointing the person and myself. Even seeing breakthroughs was not enough to change this deeply felt default position. I was stuck, for a long time. But deep down I knew I was born for this. Miracles were important.

Then I heard about Bethel (Redding, California). This was reportedly a place where healings were frequent and done by regular people in shops and car parks. This I had to see. I didn't want a conference. I wanted to see a church activated. I went for a week with my good friend and fellow elder Nick Treadgold. My goodness, what had we found? On several occasions I couldn't speak, my brain was in overdrive trying to figure out what I was seeing and hearing. As my dear friend and church leader Pete Carter said, he went to Bethel to see miracles and he found God. We found God, a culture and a level of expectation I had never seen. We chatted to a retired surgeon who had moved down from Seattle to volunteer in their healing rooms and he was so excited. He had just prayed for an eleven-year-old girl who was blind in one eye and her sight was restored. Testimonies of miracles were everywhere; they were welcomed and celebrated; they were central. Being in that atmosphere changed me.

I came home and in my heart I said "I'm going for this again." After over fifteen years of hiding in my disappointment I got my hope back in the realm of healing. On the first Sunday I was back I called people forward for healing. No one came, not one. There was no expectation in the room. The problem wasn't a lack of sick people. I'd affected them with my disappointment. A few minutes after the end of the meeting one of our young guys came up to me and said there was a new person in the queue for coffee who had injured his back at work and may be open to prayer. I didn't hesitate, I asked him if I could pray while he was in the queue. He said yes and he was immediately healed. Suddenly the people standing either side of him said they had stuff for prayer too. One had a shin splint and that got healed, another had knee problems and that got better for a while. That night in our leaders' meeting one of our leaders who was in her fifties asked for prayer for knee problems; she got healed and went for a run, no problem. For the last nine years we've been going for it. Healings have been happening at no less than one a week for that entire period. We sometimes don't have time for all the testimonies. Healings in chip shops, supermarkets and church meetings. Incurable things are healed, eyesight and hearing are restored, and increasingly people are getting healed that we haven't even prayed for. They just get healed listening to a sermon, being in a meeting. Sometimes we just ask people who came to a meeting in pain to check if the pain is still there, and they find they are healed without prayer. When we had seen about 250 healings we started a supernatural school to equip others. The school, in its seventh year at the time of writing, has seen scores of healings through its students, often in the marketplace and in full view of onlookers.

I got my hope back.

1.6 Escape the Malaise

I discovered the malaise I was in and some of the responses I had learned in Charismatic Christianity were unhelpful and even obstructing the cause of seeing the miraculous.

My culture was suspicious of the supernatural. It was truly materialistic, in that it trusted the material but was sceptical and untrusting of the unseen and the inexplicable. I can't explain or control the mechanics of healing and yet I am a vital player in seeing healing come to others. This is uncomfortable to one steeped in the value of the measurable and observable. The scientific model I grew up with said life was observable and functioned by cause and effect. These causes and effects could be seen, monitored, measured, and of course controlled. I couldn't see the cause, only the effect, and had no idea how one connected to the other! I was in the realm of uncomfortable mystery.

There was a strong set of internal reactions in me that had been formed through Christian experience and teaching and a lifetime in secular culture. Here's some of what I and our church have been seeking to learn to unlearn.

<u>1) God's unseen realm is the highest reality...</u>
...and can be trusted. Supernatural occurrences can be trusted. Testing and weighing from a place of faith and trust is different to scepticism. I have to put to death scepticism

about the things of God, because scepticism is a work of the flesh, not a fruit of the Spirit. Love believes all things, so my love for Him positions me to believe rather than doubt. The natural observable universe originated from Him who is Spirit by a word. Heaven is the superior reality; the activities there have sway over what is here in the natural universe. Jesus is head over it all. He is both creator and sustainer of the cosmos, so it bows to Him (Colossians 1:15-20; Colossians 3:1-2).

Cultivating trust as a primary reaction is so vital and is rooted in a proper view of who He is. Concern for proof, concern about the fake and deceptive, had robbed me of trust in the One who loves to display that His reality supersedes our earthly one. He is the One for whom nothing is impossible. (I am not saying measurement and verification aren't important.)

2) Learning to truly value the inexplicable activities

If we put all miraculous activity in a box marked "sovereign act of a sovereign God," we will fail to cultivate that activity among us because it just "happened" and we have no responsibility either for it happening to start with or for seeing it stewarded. Miracles are signs and wonders; they are gifts from the Father. There is a place for analysis, but not one that puts my analysis above His activity.

In the parable of the talents the one who used what he had, who valued it enough to work with it, got more. So we looked for ways to express value and pleasure in God's activity. We give testimony and we praise, often loudly. We are training ourselves to respond with delight to the activities of God. We assume it's God and check things out later rather than assuming it might not be authentic and waiting and analysing and missing the moment.

3) No Longer Aloof: Trade in Your Detachment

Analysis that keeps me aloof from the activity of heaven can mean I miss one of the great purposes of miracles. Miracles invite us into relationship with the miracle worker (Jesus). They touch us in a deep place, often bypassing the analytical and impacting the heart, because they display His heart of love. In Luke 5 when they land the miraculous catch of fish, something happens inside Peter and he exclaims, *"Depart from me, for I am a sinful man."* The overwhelming nature of supply pulls a cry from Peter's heart. Being that close to a display of goodness is meant to affect us.

Jesus expects us to learn from what He displays. He expects our faith levels to rise as the result of gleaning all the goodness we can from what He has done in front of us. When the disciples were in the boat and had forgotten bread, Jesus tries to teach them about the leaven of the Pharisees and Herod. Thinking He is talking about actual bread, they discuss among themselves the problem of lunch. They have just seen the feeding of the 4,000 and before that the feeding of the 5,000. We pick up the story in Mark 8:17:

> *"Why are you discussing the fact that you have no bread? Do you not yet perceive or understand? Are your hearts hardened? Having eyes do you not see, and having ears do you not hear? And do you not remember? When I broke the five loaves for the five thousand, how many baskets full of broken pieces did you take up?" They said to him, "Twelve." "And the seven for the four thousand, how many baskets full of broken pieces did you take up?" And they said to him, "Seven." And he said to them, "Do you not yet understand?"*

I think he was expecting them to take notice of what had happened, to understand it and to be able to reproduce it on some scale. The absence of bread should not be a problem for them, as they had already seen Jesus abundantly supply when they and the crowds were hungry. They had not valued these experiences enough to let them change their hearts. They weren't engaged. We are learning to actively engage. What is the sign telling us? What is it pointing to? We are trading our detachment for a posture of pressing in to understand the "signs" He does.

4) Ditch the "impress me" mindset

We are also working to overcome our internal proclivity to wait for the major before celebrating the minor. I said to God one day that I would get really excited when I saw three people get out of wheelchairs. He said I would see three people get out of wheelchairs as I learned to appreciate joint pain leaving, headaches healed and other so-called "lesser" miracles. He was fingering my "Go on, God, I'm waiting for you to impress me" attitude. God is not some comedian for whom I am waiting to see if he can make me laugh – "Is he good enough to stir a reaction?" He isn't my entertainer, needing to come up with bigger special effects to get me excited. He is good and He doesn't need to prove it to me. It's my responsibility to celebrate and enjoy every bit of that goodness I see, and to give thanks because He is good.

My "audience mentality," my superior scientific and somewhat sceptical stance were separating me from the wonder and value of signs and wonders.

5) Miracles are to be remembered

In the early months of our breakthroughs I wrote down everything that happened. In the process of recording and then bringing testimony I realised how easily I forgot good things. I had to strain to access them and pull them to the forefront of my mind. Many of our team were the same and we realised we had been trained in a culture of bad news. I found in many leaders' meetings we were more comfortable talking about challenges and problems, perhaps because they were our daily fare. I've even seen people get offended if you harped on about all the miracles. I began to see that the culture I was living in, which values facing "reality," often means we miss His reality, His display of goodness.

I realised I couldn't remember good things as easily as bad. So we recorded them, testified about them and every leaders' meeting now starts with good news. We are training ourselves out of our western culture, and at times it feels unnatural and uncomfortable, but that isn't because it's unbiblical; it's because we have been marinated in negativity for so long that negative feels normal. Our defaults are being reprogrammed; we are changing our normal. To steward God's activity well requires a recalibration of our thought life to "forget not" all His benefits (Psalm 103).

6) I'm in control of my hope

Disappointments come and they may be big. We have those in abundance too. But that doesn't have to equal a sick heart, which is what I suffered from for a long time. It's hope deferred that makes the heart sick (more of that in the chapter on hope). Too many people are afraid of disappointing others if they offer prayer and nothing happens. The pastorally gifted are particularly prone to keeping people free from the pain of disappointments. We face this all the time, and have come to these conclusions:

a) People generally feel loved when they are prayed for;
b) It's better to have an atmosphere where healing is reached for and expected, because more get healed and believe for it, than in a culture where this is not pursued.

An atmosphere of faith can attract sick people because it's a place where something can happen.

7) Celebrate others' breakthroughs

Let's assume for a minute you are longing to see someone healed through your prayer. One by one ALL your friends see people healed. You secretly know that one or two of these friends aren't walking as humbly with the Lord as you are, and you know for sure they haven't persisted as hard as you for a breakthrough. Nevertheless you are the one still waiting. You have a decision to make. You can find reasons to undermine your friends' successes. You can be grumpy with God in an "it's not fair" kind of a way. You can give up, based on it not being fair. Or you can rejoice with those who rejoice. I can get them to pray for me for an impartation so that I move in that same level. Every time I have to choose I am going to be happy, I am going to celebrate Jesus and encourage the person who just saw the breakthrough I have been longing for. I choose to say no to envy, no to insecurity and competition. As our friend and prophet Julian Adams loves to say, it's time to get your "crazy praise on." It's not about me, it's about Him, and He is getting glory through my friends. Isn't that awesome!

8) Deal with Fear

As long as I'm walking in fear I am not walking in love, for love casts out fear. Love is vital, for faith works through love. Fear can come in many forms. God can be moving in people around you in dramatic ways and you feel afraid He doesn't love you because all you are manifesting is steadfastness. You can get into fear that He will never touch you, and that in itself is paralysing. You can be afraid of things being fake, or afraid of being swept up and out of control.

When God is doing visible, measurable things around us,

they can give us external checkpoints to measure ourselves against. To those of us who feel fearful and insecure this can be bad news. Each one of us needs to find a place where we are secure in His love and our identity. If we react from insecurity and so become envious, critical or cynical we can actually infect the atmosphere negatively as well as insulate ourselves. Remember:

> *If you then, who are evil, know how to give good gifts to your children, how much more will the heavenly Father give the* **Holy Spirit** *to those who ask him. Luke 11:13*

In other words, He's a good Father!

There is a genuine fear of being out of control that affects many people, and it rather pinpoints a key issue of faith for us.

First, God the Holy Spirit does not sweep you along without your cooperation. We are co-labourers with Him, sons, not servants to be moved around at His whim. The Holy Spirit isn't an impersonal force bashing into you or through you, He is a person who loves you, a friend (2 Corinthians 13:14). Demonic spirits possess us, ultimately overruling our better inclinations. Holy Spirit requires your permission. That permission can look like hunger and thirst for Him, or it can look like a forthright conversation with Him.

Second, God wants to do you good and only good. Trust and yield to His good and best intentions for your life and fear will leave your heart. So, sometimes God sweeps in and does things you didn't think you gave Him permission to do – He is just being good to you!

Prophecies and tongues gave the church some challenges all those years ago in the Charismatic renewal. Now we have visions, trances, angels, healings, and some things we have no category for?! The opportunities for fear and confusion are numerous.

<ins>Supernatural is Essential</ins>

We are realising in our experience that the apostle Paul's success was rooted in the fact that signs and wonders produced obedience in people (Romans 15:18). The demonstration of good news is at least as essential as proclaiming it.

But to enjoy more of these things requires that they are valued and celebrated as the gifts they are from our Father. To treat them suspiciously or with undue caution is like burying your talent in a field. What's exciting is that the Father adds more to what you steward well; He comes and adds increase to your increase. What you ignore or bury because you are afraid or don't understand is ultimately lost. Read Matthew 25:25. At the end of the parable the guy with the single talent says, *"...so I was **afraid**, and I went and hid your talent in the ground. Here you have what is yours."* Fear can make you freeze and do nothing with your gift or talent. Fear can keep us from our destiny as profoundly supernatural believers.

1.7 Building Good Values

Just as I had to go through a process of rewiring, so we are in the process of helping our church value God's miracle intervention. For us it means steadily doing away with scepticism and moving to celebration. We've worked on this in a number of ways.

We can't just keep doing and behaving as we did when not much was happening and expect results. Part of the reason not much was happening was our culture:

a) Through teaching and rooting experiences in scripture, people start to trust what God is doing. At first people can be excited or cautious about the supernatural. Both camps tend to call everything they don't understand "weird." Over time, however, we are seeking for His normal to become our normal, not our weird. The Bible is essentially a supernatural book, and full of miraculous stories that help us navigate our current experiences. Finding biblical help builds trust and security. I am constantly surprised by how much "weird" stuff is in the Bible... God lifted Ezekiel by his hair!

b) We deliberately express value for what He does supernaturally through testimony and sharing good news. Our motivation is not to "show off" but to show Him off to all. Hidden breakthroughs don't give much glory to God. I would suggest if He healed you it was for two reasons: 1. Your wellbeing, which he deeply cares about; 2. His glory, so please, no false modesty where you don't share what He has done for you; it's not just about you. We emphasise miracle testimonies, because that is the area we need to strengthen the most. Testimony and celebration of heaven's activity show the Lord our delight in what He is doing. We are treasuring the good things He is showing us. So we clap and cheer and give space for the supernatural stories.

Get this growing in church community life and you have a breeding ground for hope and breakthrough.

<u>Growing a supernatural culture gives us an export</u>
As we generate good news and a good news culture, we can then be a source of hope to a world which is drowning in its own body weight of bad news. Think of all the movies

about a dystopian future. Think of the world we are living in; there's the fear of global warming, young adults have little hope of buying a house, there is fear of another future financial meltdown and global terrorism threats. Does anyone have hope? We do, and at many levels. Bad news might sell, but it's good news that transforms. Our gloom is to be as the midday sun compared to everyone else's. We are arising and shining when we display hope to the world. We do this by displaying and celebrating the good news of the invasion of the Kingdom of God.

It's impossible for God to move and the Holy Spirit to work and for hope not to be renewed (Romans 15:13). When we start to hope vibrantly in our church communities we become exporters of hope to our streets, cities and nations.

1.8 Miracles: Our Best Argument

I spent a good deal of time reading some books on Christian apologetics. They were written by brilliant people. All were pretty much based on the scripture in 1 Peter that exhorts us to be ready to give a reason for our faith. We do need this, and our children need it. But we have a more persuasive argument to present. Take a look at Jesus' responses to the need for proof.

> Jesus answered them, "I told you, and you do not believe. <u>The works that I do in my Father's name bear witness about me,</u> but you do not believe because you are not part of my flock. My sheep hear my voice, and I know them, and they follow me. I give them eternal life, and they will never perish, and no one will snatch them out of my hand. My Father, who has given them to me, is greater than all, and no one is able to snatch them out of the Father's hand. I and the Father are one." The Jews

picked up stones again to stone him. Jesus answered them, "<u>I have shown you many good works from the Father</u>; for which of them are you going to stone me?" John 10:25-32

"If I am not doing the works of my Father, then do not believe me; but if I do them, even though you do not believe me, believe the works, that you may know and understand that the Father is in me and I am in the Father." John 10:37-38

"Believe me that I am in the Father and the Father is in me, or else believe on account of the works themselves." John 14:11

Jesus used the miracles He did as proof of who He was. They were allowed to not believe in Him if He didn't do the Father's works. They were encouraged to believe on the basis of the miraculous works alone. What's surprising is that He doesn't appeal to His excellent teaching or logic; He doesn't even appeal to His amazing character. This is because the miracles displayed the nature of the Father. If you saw Jesus, you had seen the Father, not just heard a message about the Father.

As the Church, the people of God, we have no better calling card than the one Jesus used. No other methodology was left us. We have made up a few of our own along the way because we didn't see many miracles. We often substituted rational argument for miraculous display. The unbelieving world has been given permission by Jesus to not believe us if we don't do the works of the Father.

We are returning to the use of the original calling card, the original apologetic, which is signs and wonders. Experiences change people's thinking faster and more easily than rational argument, no matter how good the argument, or the arguer. There are always two sides in a discussion, and pride to be defended, not just the facts. But when God breaks in, all other voices are silenced; the invasion of the unseen changes the nature of the whole debate.

We are called to be conformed to the image of Christ. So often I read that, and what I thought I was reading was "be like Him in character." What He is saying is in fact holistic. Be conformed to His image in every way, with signs and wonders and good character. Do the works He did and greater works because He has gone to the Father. We are explicitly included in the dispensing of healing and the power of God. How can we presume to come up with better tools than the ones He used? How can we assume we can survive well without the strategies He used and in turn bequeathed to us? These things are our inheritance. The supernatural is the new normal for the children of God. We are sons of the same kind as Jesus, not some lesser breed.

Miracles Demonstrate the Intimacy Jesus Had with the Father

That they may know and understand that the Father is in me and I am in the Father. John 10:38

Our intimate connection to God is so vital to this whole realm. Every attempt to convince us that we are disconnected from the union we have with the Father's heart and affection, from His Spirit and His affirmation, is to be resisted with vigour. We are in Him and He is in us and we are in the Father. We can actively enjoy that reality through abiding in Him, cultivating the relationship already supplied, drawing on His nourishing heart and His infinite resources through our intimacy with Him; that's where the miraculous flows from in Jesus and we function just the same.

Miracles Bring Understanding

> ...that you may know and understand... John 10:38

Knowing and understanding come from believing the miraculous works.

This was a foreign idea to me. I was used to knowing through learning, lectures, books and Bible teachers. But there are nutrients in miracles. God is saying something and not just doing something when He does a miracle. This breaks down our western boxes, our categories that say: books are for learning, miracles are for healing people, not teaching me something. When people started getting healed in my preaching I felt there was a message, something to be pursued, an invitation even. He started it, but He wanted me to press in and accept the invitation to then take the risk of initiating healing without prayer. I learned from what He did. Why would He do that when He said lay hands on the sick? Many were healed when Peter's shadow fell on them, so I figure I am learning the faith to see my presence in a room be enough, because of His presence in me and with me.

You see and feel love in miracles. You experience and see power in miracles. This is beyond knowing the truth in your head that He is powerful and loving.

Miracles Build Faith

> ...and my speech and my message were not in plausible words of wisdom, but in demonstration of the Spirit and of power, that your faith might not rest in the wisdom of men but in the power of God. 1 Corinthians 2:4-5

Faith has a deeper resting place than reason. Demonstrations of power create a space in the heart where faith can rest more unshakably than that formed from words and rational learning alone. Seeing works of power is a way that faith rests in and on the wisdom of God.

I know you're thinking "faith comes from hearing," and of course that is true, but it's not the whole picture. Faith does in this case come from experiencing!

Miracles Display the Father's Nature

Jesus said "If you have seen me you have seen the Father," "I and the Father are one," "I only do what I see the Father doing." Around one-third of the gospel material covers the miraculous and healing. John says in effect that this is only a small sample because the world couldn't contain the books if everything were written down, and that's in three years of ministry. It would be a mistake to view His whole ministry through the lens of the incident at the pool of Siloam where He clearly ignores many sick people to heal the one. If you study the gospels you find most often Jesus' order of service was to heal all the sick present and then do the teaching.

I got the idea from somewhere that only doing what the Father was doing was straining to discern the one thing He was up to in a room or a street. Jesus shows us it's the opposite, it's hard to keep up with all the Father is doing. He loves healing sick people. This tells us about His will and His heart and His nature. If you touched Jesus you got well; if you touch God you get well. Those who touched Jesus believing they would be well had healing virtue flow into their lives, and this came from the heart of the Father of Healing. Jesus and the Father are one. Never did Jesus say to someone "I won't heal you. It's not the Father's will" (More on this in the section on Healing in Part 4).

1.9 Honour the Key to Revival

A long time ago, God showed me the scripture below. It happened as I was seeking greater breakthrough in the realm of healing. I was shocked to find that Jesus, the Son of God, anointed with limitless amounts of the Holy Spirit, could be limited by the reception He got!

> ...and coming to his home town he taught them in their synagogue, so that they were astonished, and said, "Where did this man get this wisdom and these mighty works? Is not this the carpenter's son? Is not his mother called Mary? And are not his brothers James and Joseph and Simon and Judas? And are not all his sisters with us? Where then did this man get all these things?" And they **took offence** at him. But Jesus said to them, "A prophet is not without **honour** except in his home town and in his own household." And he did not do many mighty works there, because of their **unbelief.**
> Matthew 13:54-58

I preached a message on it in the church I was leading at the time. There just happened to be a mature and nationally recognised prophet in the meeting that day. He came up to me afterward and said he thought that was a key message for our nation. Wow, what do you do with that?! In that season God spoke to me and said that prayer isn't the key to revival in the UK. Honour is. He said "Plenty of prayer is taking place, but the capacity of the people in the church to receive the people I'm going to use as revival catalysts is limited, and so the work I can do is limited."

When I first saw this, I had no place in my mind or experience for it to rest or find practical expression. I thought God was sovereign, and of course He is, but how can sovereignty be overturned by humanity? Surely if God wanted to heal and do mighty works, nothing on earth could stop Him. This scripture and its parallel passages in Mark and Luke were saying something different.

After receiving this revelation, every time I heard a leader well honoured in public it would make me cry. I can remember the first time it happened at a large conference I was attending. Some wonderful visiting speaker honoured a woman called Eileen Wallis, wife of late author, leader and speaker Arthur Wallis. The room erupted in applause and some cheering, and I was undone. Whenever that has happened in an authentic way since, the same thing happens.

Of course this can be done in a plastic and superficial way. That has no effect on me, nor should it. But when people find genuine affection and value in their hearts for others and express it, I find it incredibly moving. I think it's the heart of God. He celebrates us all profusely.

I have seen many unhealthy versions of honour. I also saw a running away from it in case it became abused. I knew it was true, but didn't know what it looked like. The first time I encountered a healthy version was my first visit to Bethel Church in Redding California. Honour was a cultural reality, not just some superficial applause for a leader. But people's honour for people was everywhere – everyone was honoured. It was an atmosphere with very little judgement. There's a set of attitudes behind this culture that is costly to develop for people brought up in cynicism and scepticism. I recognised that I needed reprogramming.

In our passage above, Jesus helps us; here He links offence, honour and faith/unbelief.

He says in effect, if you are offended by someone because you think they are a bit too big for their boots, someone who was just like you and now is knocking it out of the park in the public arena, you can limit their function in God.

He is saying if you are suspicious of how they got what they got because you knew them and they weren't like that when you knew them, you can limit what you and others can receive from them.

If you are so familiar with them and their family that you can only see them through the lens of familiarity, you are judging them and so limiting their effect in and around you.

If you have so locked them into your old experience of them that, despite reports from elsewhere, you can't let go of that view, your limited experience of them now is because of the limits you are imposing, not their limitations.

He is saying if you can't let people you know become extraordinary, because you know you are the same as them and in your history with them you were their equal, and you think "I am as good as them," you have trapped them in the past. If your need for equality means they can't become more prominent or effective than you, you will receive from them the old version you hold in your heart, not the reality stood in front of you.

You only get out of them what you value in them! Familiarity, judging the book by the cover, wanting to think you are as good as anybody else, can put a limitation on what God can deliver to your life and the community around you.

In His home town there was a collective effect, a group effect. Enough people there had these poor attitudes that they created an atmosphere that limited what He could do for them all. They created an atmosphere inside which God was limited. That means my attitude can contribute to my friends not receiving from God what they need! Ouch! It means there's a God-sized delivery for you, stood in front of you, and you only get the human-sized one.

A positive posture of heart toward people is honour. Jesus was identifying this as the missing piece in Nazareth. Honour is fundamentally "to value." It is a judgement; but a positive one. They didn't value Jesus and God didn't step in to make them value Him. They stumbled over the ordinary boy doing the extraordinary as a man. Jesus says this is unbelief, plain and simple. They didn't believe who He was. In other places people just had to touch Him to be healed. This crowd could have leaned on Him all day and got nothing. Honour displaces offence and catalyses faith in its place.

Honour is the key to revival.

1.10 Your Worst Nightmare

What would be your nightmare – the worst person you could imagine releasing revival to your city, whose meetings would you avoid? I thought about it and mine was a non-white, divorced woman with no theological training. I clearly had some repenting to do on whom God could use and issues of race, class, divorce and women in leadership, not to mention a snobby attitude about theological training! I have other issues too. I don't like scruffy people or shouty people, or people with a poor ministry track record. God help me if He uses a scruffy loud person with a dodgy ministry history. But what if her history had brought her to a place of unique dependence on God? What if her appearance worked for where she was reaching? What if God liked the way she talked? Without serious repentance I am stuffed! Revival could pass me by if it comes in a package not approved by my good self.

I have found revivalists are amazing people, often very focused and determined. They can be clear, even a bit blunt and unwilling to change the subject. They know there's an enemy trying to dilute our impact and blunt our edge. Obtaining supernatural breakthrough is getting easier, but for many of them it is and has been a challenging journey through disappointments and unanswered questions; learning to renew their minds from natural thinking to supernatural thinking to get to the place where they can bring release to captives. They have to press through others' misunderstandings of them and often judgements about their motives; it can be an uncomfortable quest. So the package they come in varies, and is not to everyone's taste; and if you are prone to judge, they will probably step on that button in you at some point. Revivalists take risks, and by definition not every risk ends with success, or even looks sensible. In the realm of risk there is a fine line between genius and idiot! Let's honour the fire-carriers, the revivalists and supernatural catalysts, who are paying a price to raise the level for all of us.

How about applauding mistakes that have been made from a heart of faith that's willing to take a risk to move the agenda forward?

Can Anything Good Come Out of Nazareth?

What if the good people of downtown Nazareth had responded differently? What if their attitude had been "Jesus, we remember you – you made pretty decent kitchen cabinets back in the day – and we see you are doing some mighty stuff you didn't learn from your (earthly) dad. Please show us, you mean a lot to us; come on, be awesome, we want your success; let's celebrate Him, everyone! Jesus, who left as a carpenter, is doing miracles and saying amazing stuff – let's welcome Him as a great son of our town. He is honouring our town, He will forever be known as Jesus of Nazareth!" What if they had loved Jesus? Loved in the Bible sense of "rejoicing in the truth, hoping and believing all things" (1 Corinthians 13). They missed a trick. They could have been more than a birthplace; they could have been a place that cheered Him on and were famous for their reception of Him and their encouragement of Him. Their chosen attitude was poor and created an atmosphere that limited Jesus. No wonder it was said "Can anything good come out of Nazareth?"

We have something to learn: to perceive and so to value the Jesus in each of us. We need to learn to do this to each of our friends, our family, ministry colleagues and church leaders, in fact each functioning part of the body of Christ. Let's go large and give this kind of treatment to each person made in the image of God.

Maintaining an internal posture of honour toward others makes a larger space inside us to receive what they have for us from God. It also activates their gifts, helping them to operate at a higher level toward us. The outcome is strengthening, it builds spiritual momentum in us, and if it becomes cultural, it builds a larger spiritual momentum in which all gifts can flourish and have impact. Honour is the key to revival.

What does the journey to this different atmosphere look like?

1.11 Love is Fierce

Love is a big deal. No one word can adequately describe it. But *fierce* will do for now, not because He's scary particularly, but because his love burns, is relentless, passionate, focused, as well as full of affection, kind and gentle; it never stops and can't be outrun; it consumes darkness and is completely without fear. Yet it's so intense it produces reverence, a holy fear if you like.

As I write this chapter I am very aware that because this is a book I can sound like an expert, and I want you to know that definitely isn't true. Everything here in this chapter is either a work in progress or a lesson painfully learned.

Thousands have left the church because of the damage done through control and manipulation. This culture is literally killing us!

Oh, how I wish love was just a warm fuzzy feeling; something that happens easily because all the people around me are basically wonderful and deserving of my love. I like them, they get me and I get them. If that were love, no child would be consistently loved, because they act up and misbehave and all the warm fuzzies disappear quite fast! Especially at three in the morning.

> *If I speak in the tongues of men and of angels, but have not love, I am a noisy gong or a clanging cymbal. And if I have prophetic powers, and understand all mysteries and all knowledge, and if I have all faith, so as to remove mountains, but have not love, I am nothing. If I give away all I have, and if I deliver up my body to be burned, but have not love, I gain nothing.*
>
> *Love is patient and kind; love does not envy or boast; it is not arrogant or rude. It does not insist on its own way; it is not irritable or resentful; it does not rejoice at wrongdoing, but rejoices with the truth. Love bears all things, believes all things, hopes all things, endures all things.*
>
> *Love never ends.* 1 Corinthians 13

This is not written for weddings. This was written by Paul and directed into the centre of a white-hot cauldron of charismatic activity called the Corinthian church. They had speaking in tongues in abundance, more prophecy than they knew what to do with, healings, miracles, words of wisdom and knowledge. Not to mention apostles, prophets, teachers etc. I don't think it's a corrective in the sense of "stop doing all that stuff" but a cultural tune-up, a plumb line check. Paul knew if they didn't get the core motivations and behaviours right, if they didn't keep loving in all the charismatic fire, they would be in trouble.

We need fierce love for a mighty outpouring. I think he was saying something like:

Patience is needed in an environment where instant miracles happen and yours isn't happening. It's needed when it's confusing because the revelations don't piece together or the community appears to be chaotic; patience to wait for clarity and understanding and breakthrough.

Kindness is needed when you know how powerfully God just used you, and your friend remains sick in the midst of the miracles. Kindness is needed in the way ministry is done, especially if God just seems to be blessing everything, no matter how it's done.

I choose not to envy the guy who does the most amazing miracles. I choose not to cover my envy with a cloak of acceptability by saying I am just being cautious, looking at the state of the guy's life, i.e. a reason for my caution.

As the guy who just raised the dead for the third time I choose not to boast in anything except Jesus Christ. I choose to use my newfound significance to make others look brilliant.

No matter how brilliantly I am used, I powerfully choose not to let it go to my head and I stay teachable, I remain a learner, and I will learn from anyone who has something from God. I will submit to others and other gifts. I serve other people.

I don't use powerful leadership gifts to dominate others. In His love I deal with the temptations to do the non-love "command and control" thing and overcome it in Jesus' name. I'm a good listener and I know there are other views that have value, even though I am feeling like His number one awesome hero right now!

I'm not rejoicing when there's failure, especially if those failures mean new opportunities for me, and they prove I was right all along.

I'm not listening to tales, gossip or complaint. I celebrate truth – truth about people, truth from God. I celebrate it by having true relationships, not polluted by what others told me about you. I'm true because I tell you the truth about me and the truth about you. And the truth about you is the truth of how Father sees you.

Bearing all things can look like carrying the late adopters with you in the fire of revival, looking after the vulnerable when the vision is exploding and there is so much to do.

Believing all things doesn't mean believing anything about anybody, but believing the best. Keep believing in people around you. Keep believing for people around you.

Hoping all things is part of what this book is about. Despite appearances, circumstances or even experiences that would attempt to dash hope, we don't let it die; we allow hope to bubble up again and again to rule in our expectations.

You wouldn't think much endurance was required in a revival outpouring. But as the Corinthian church demonstrates, there was a great deal of imperfection to be ironed out in the midst of all the charismatic flow. There was immorality, division and selfishness at communion time. You needed endurance and abounding hope in the midst of all that.

When there's fire in the house our hearts need strengthening with inner power to know the height of his love and express it to one another. We can't be seduced by power itself to abandon love for one another by making more power the only goal. Displays of power can trigger mixed motives in the best of people.

You get the idea. Spiritual power is sustained by a radical commitment to love. Paul wants the power to flow and the problems of the community solved, so he exhorts them to a culture of love; higher attitudes than mere human ones, attitudes fuelled by the same power that is being displayed in the outpouring of charismatic life.

In this environment of glorious Holy Spirit imperfection, we give up any right we may feel we have to judge others, speak ill of others, criticise others, or believe the worst of others. And we fight for truth. We celebrate and rejoice over the truth about other people, and we keep believing, keep hoping and stay connected.

Love doesn't happen in isolation. It needs a context, a community, other people to express it to. Paul is speaking to the context of a gloriously diverse church community.

The context for this exhortation to love is also diversity, which should tell us something. Love really gets to show itself when we are around people who are not like us. I have noticed a drift toward small churches, small gatherings, often of like-minded people. There can also be a proliferation of ministries that are about one thing, that represent just one gift. But what good is an eye if it's not in a body? The point of an eye is that it travels with the body it's in. It doesn't just observe and see, it lives the consequences with the rest of the body. It sees where you are going and goes there with you!

There is much less pull on love when you mix with people who are like you in gift and temperament. It's easier to love when the diversity is limited to the few mates that fit in your lounge, who would probably be your friends anyway. One of the glories of the body of Christ is its many-faceted nature, unity in extreme diversity. Love is proven in close proximity to difference, not in distant appreciation. As my old pastor used to say, "When Jesus comes into your life, he brings **all** his friends with Him."

<u>Diluted, polluted, misunderstood, hijacked</u>

Love has been made to mean sex, liking things, affection, even personal preference. For example: I really love strawberry ice cream more than vanilla. What Paul is talking about, what the church is increasingly grappling with and producing, is the thing that made the universe and motivated salvation; it's something so powerful that no other created power or being can separate us from it. This has to be more profound than my emotions toward ice cream.

When someone says "there's not enough love in this church" you know they have turned its definition on its head, moved it from "what am I giving" to "what am I receiving," moved it from "how do I bless?" to a judgement on others' skill at blessing.

It really feels like we have to fight for love. Of course, I don't mean fight for God's love. That is freely, passionately given to each of us. I mean to wrestle with the idea, wrestle to express the authentic, to create community atmospheres that are full of honour and celebration of one another, full of mutual submission and blessing of one another.

<u>What does love look like?</u>

The simple answer is it looks like God because God is love. But there's a journey for us as we leave worldly distortion and seek to recover the real 'God thing' called love.

I can't remember the source of this, but someone from an older generation said that in their day if something broke, they fixed it, they didn't buy a new one. Really that's the heart of covenant: it's a commitment, which has to be mutual, to keep fixing the relationship and not throw it away.

In modern consumer culture it is actually quicker and cheaper to get a new one. People aren't products, though, and disposable relationships can look attractive but are actually more costly and damaging.

In my experience, and I have some painful ones like we all do, relationships end because they are not truly mutual. Both parties have to see their responsibilities, be willing to be wrong at times and be good at putting things right. No side should see itself as superior to the other. Without mutual submission it doesn't work. When there is a major breakdown it's never all one side, but there is often unwillingness by one party to step into the other's shoes; instead there is a determination to hold their feet to the fire until they get the point. The belief we can hold is "I can make them change," and that just isn't true. I'm in control of me, not them.

Sometimes we don't "get" what our friends are trying to tell us. At this point there are decisions both parties need to make. If something profound really does need to be faced up to, it has to feel safe to explore the issue apart from judgement and agenda. You have to know these are faithful wounds, from faithful friends, not words in anger or words attached to agendas. My experience is that if I sniff an agenda, I can't own the problem the friend says I have. It's not safe to go there. Truth is required on all sides, truthful approaches and responses.

If someone you love is struggling to see something, and you know it's hurting them, it's hard not to speak. Being received is the goal, however, not getting the issue of your chest. So finding ways to give the friend the security that you are not going to give up on them is vital. That safe place makes deeper discoveries possible.

What's the point? The point is that true change through relationship can only happen in the safety of covenant relationships. These kinds of relationships are characterised by the commitment to not quit and a genuine commitment to the benefit of the other people in the relationship. I am not looking for personal gain, revenge, point-scoring or forcing change, I am looking for the benefit of the other. I am looking for deeper connection with my friend.

<u>Fanning the flames</u>

Nothing sucks the life out of a move of God more than division, broken relationships and dishonour.

Keeping love alive and looking for the value in people fans the flames of revival and keeps them burning. It opens a doorway for you to receive powerful things from the person right in front of you.

Honour is the key to revival and love is a big key to sustaining it.

Note

I want to point you to some other resources that give this topic a more excellent treatment than I can here. Danny Silk's materials on "Keep Your Love On" are brilliant, and his workshops and online resources are extremely helpful to us all as we seek to recover love.

PART 2

ONLY HUMAN?

"You are who you think you are. But you're not who you think you are…unless your thoughts are His." A riddle, or a clue?

Our sense of identity radically affects our intimacy.

Our intimacy profoundly affects our identity.

Who we think we are affects what we do.

2.1 Finding Myself in the Kitchen

One day I was walking into our kitchen, and no one else was around. I had just discovered some poor financial news that would affect us as a family, something I perhaps could have prevented if I had been more aware. "You're such an idiot!" I exclaimed out loud. Immediately I sensed this strong inner voice rebuke me and say "Don't talk about yourself like that…" short pause "…in fact, don't talk about what I have made like that."

This was so against the mood I was in, it had to be Holy Spirit; I couldn't be making it up right now. This experience happened at the end of the season I described earlier, a season of what seemed to be unrelenting bad news, and I was feeling a fool for steering my life into such a crazy set of circumstances.

Those words and the inner sense that accompanied them stopped me in my tracks. I have to say I was a bit dumbfounded. The words I had spoken had gushed out of some strong emotion; the words He said stopped the momentum of those feelings. Didn't God realise whom He was speaking to and what had been happening? *I have the evidence in front of me, God, that proves that what I think of me is actually true, hadn't You noticed this great pile of FACTS?* But this was God, and He kindly but profoundly disagreed with my assessment of me and my pile of proof.

What I looked like through His eyes was significantly different from my personal assessment of myself. I thought I was being real; He thought I was being damning of His creation and dishonouring His perspective.

This was part of a journey into realising He consistently differed with me over the matter of my identity, and one of a series of debates on the subject I was, happily, losing.

A little while later He said, "What's going to wreck you as you have deeper encounters with Me is My high opinion of you." What? God said this!? I was in worship at our Supernatural School (Hope School of Supernatural Life) and God said, in effect, that getting in touch with Him in a deeper way would create some kind of positive emotional meltdown. I would be so impacted by how He celebrated me, loved who I was and more, that it would take me beyond the boundaries of my current emotional capacities.

My expectation had been that nearness would involve me becoming more aware of my sin and lack. I had read about Smith Wigglesworth, who lived in an atmosphere of the Presence that "few men could stand in." I wanted it, but was scared; scared of exposure and conviction, scared of finding "ugly me." The words of revelation turned my expectation and theology upside down. What would be hard to handle was the extreme positivity I would experience in high levels of intimacy.

Only Human?

People really praising you and celebrating you can mess with your head. A bit of encouragement is nice, but when it gets more ramped up – if you're like me – it starts to create anxiety. *Can I deliver? They think I'm more amazing than I do. This is confusing, and where are these ideas coming from?* It can actually trigger a withdrawal instinct in me because I'm afraid I will disappoint them when they find out what I'm really like. So I internally engage reverse and back off. But Heavenly Dad knows me totally; He has zero illusions about me, it's impossible for Him to be unrealistic about me, and He is perfect in His judgements. Taking all this into account, knowing and weighing every fact and being unaware of nothing, God our Father is supercharged encouragement. He's our biggest fan and the one who celebrates us under the influence of extreme emotions! (Zephaniah 3:17.)

Jesus illustrated this reality like this. The Kingdom of Heaven is like a merchant looking for fine pearls. (*The Father is the merchant and we are the pearls.*) When he found **one** of **great** value (*that would be you*), he went away and sold everything he had and bought it. *He gave His only Son, Jesus, as the full purchase price. And it only takes one pearl – you – to trigger the merchant – Father – to sacrificial action* (Matthew 13:45-46, *my notes added).* This is the nature of the Kingdom of Heaven and therefore the Father whose kingdom it is. He is the one who permeates its whole atmosphere and shapes its culture.

Much of what I had learned was about what I was saved from and for, saved from sin's power and penalty and saved for a life of sanctification and mission in relationship to God. What I was seeing and enjoying was what salvation had created me to be.

It wasn't just God's justice that was satisfied at the cross, but also, and more importantly, His Father heart was expressed and exposed for all to see. His pent-up desires for His sons to be able to come home was satisfied. Open connection to His earthly family was now possible without the paraphernalia of ceremony and sacrifice, law-keeping and priests. The Father had sons, Jesus had brothers, family was bought back home (Hebrews 12:23; Hebrews 2:10-11).

2.2 Who "I am"

We make so many "I am" statements – statements that reveal who we really think we are. "I'm not a great singer," "I'm not creative," and "I'm not good at maths." Some feelings run deep, our statements about ourselves verbalising convictions about our worth and significance. "I'm not worth much," "I'm hopeless." In the kitchen incident I mentioned above I said "I'm such an idiot!" These statements tell us a lot about what we think and feel on the inside.

Some of these statements reflect what we have been told by significant others in our life. Some reflect our own assessment based on our view of life's events. Some reflect a deeply held religious view that humility is truly thinking you are small and insignificant and that this is spiritual because being insignificant magnifies His greatness. The truth is God doesn't need me to be small for Him to be great.

Some personal identity statements can reflect a nation's culture – many cultures contain the idea that you mustn't get above yourself, and they are good at pulling you down if you get elevated in your thinking.

The fruit of all these influences is a deep inner conviction about who I am, and even what it is possible to think about that subject. There's a box, boundaries to acceptable thought on the subject of who you are. Then heaven comes and no box is adequate. Its culture is not riddled with such constrained thinking. His heart for us cannot be contained by our inner self-defined limits. He is breaking that box for love's sake.

Only Human?

We want to know who we are. We do psychological tests to discover ourselves; people travel the world to "find themselves"; people trace family trees – are they related to royalty, is there a mysterious link to pirates or great leaders of the past? There's an itch inside that what their life or upbringing is telling them isn't the whole story or even their ultimate reality.

As a student I took a "gap summer." Gap years weren't common back then. I had just become a Christian and was clueless about my new faith. Before my conversion I had planned this summer trip of discovery. My then girlfriend and I set off on our adventure. First stop was my artist uncle who lived in Amsterdam. He was into all sorts of spiritual stuff and, not knowing any different, off we went to join in a form of transcendental meditation. We listened to a guru and learned that because spirit and breath were related you should keep your nasal passages clean. He was also into the early days of healthy eating and not using chemicals. So I bought supplies of peppermint-based shampoo with which I fumigated the whole floor of my halls at university. Every time I washed my hair, everyone knew!

We then caught something called the "magic bus." On reflection it was magic because it got us there. It was less magic on the return journey because it broke down halfway and was irreparable. We ended up hitchhiking our way back from what was then Yugoslavia.

We wanted to see how far we could go. On the bus were people planning to get to Istanbul and even India overland. On the bus there were also a lot of drugs. It was a bus full of young people on a journey to find themselves, find themselves on a LSD trip or by visiting a guru or just by travelling and dropping out of normal life.

In those days there were borders in Europe. As we approached the German border the driver said "If you have any 'stuff,' get rid of it now. They always search us." That was not surprising as we were hardly travelling incognito. This bus had psychedelic paintwork.

Lots of anonymous-looking packets got chucked out of the window. The young man next to us said he was not going to throw away his drugs because they had cost him a lot of money. So he took his brown paper bag full of hash (marijuana) and ate it all right there. We didn't hear from him for a couple of days. He was mostly unconscious!

Somewhere in Austria the bus driver stopped and picked up a hitchhiker. He told us that the guy wasn't riding for free and had offered to pay his fare in kind. He gave the driver two tablets of "speed" for his ticket, which the driver took. We didn't stop again and we drove very fast and overtook on some very scary stretches of road. The buzz of the speed started to wear off as we parked up in Athens. The driver had reduced the journey time by many hours and was quite pleased he had offered an improved service. I was not so sure. My view on the benefit of drug-taking as a route to discovery was taking a dive!

The next leg of our journey of discovery took us to Crete. We were told there was a hippy beach in the south where you could go and sleep on the beach! How cool. So we slept on the beach and ran into the sea at sunrise; that was our shower. We used a cave for a lavatory.

(Just for interest, you can still go to that very cave, but you have to pay to enter because it's a Roman burial site. We went for free!)

We were living free and looking for meaning.

Why am I telling you this? Because the urge is strong; knowing who you are is important, it drives us places, sometimes places that aren't actually helpful. I can say the answer isn't on a drug trip or in a new diet, or a new partner. It's not in using no chemicals or breathing water up your nose to clear your airways. It's not in another country, it's in Jesus in you.

The journey we need to take is not into the nations, but into the world of our Heavenly Father's opinion. As we find who we are in Him, we then need His backing. We need the assurance of the Holy Spirit to step out into our true identity, to break with our history, our religious thought or societal pressure and into glory!

Only when we discover our true identity can we enter our destiny, and connect to our dreams. Only then do we truly hope because we connect to the hope within us.

Our life is fuelled by our sense of identity. It is vital to discover who we really are and courageously live from the shape our Father gave us. It's tempting to live in response to the need of the moment, the expectation of the crowd or even the story told us by our life so far. But we can live life from a different place: His opinion and His reality in us. Jesus who lived from who He was, not in reaction to what He experienced or what others thought.

I discovered my identity has several elements, several influences that shape the single idea, that shape the deep inner sense of who I think I am. This produces inside me convictions about what I am capable of and what I will live like. As a man thinks, so he is.

2.3 He Is in Me

It's pretty clear Jesus knew who He was (John 13:3; Philippians 2:5-6). He made a lot of "I am" statements in public. These statements now help us know who He really was – the Son of God. But how would we have felt if we were in the crowd when He proclaimed Himself to be "the way, the truth and the life"? It's easy for us who can read the accounts with hindsight, but back then it was shocking, outrageous and got Him in big trouble. How would you feel if a guest speaker showed up in your church and proclaimed he was the "resurrection and the life," or "the light of the world"?

Jesus' inner playlist, the words He heard about Himself, spoke to Himself and therefore said about Himself, was full of things many of us have never said or thought about ourselves because our logic is earthbound in a way His wasn't, and He's calling us to live His reality.

So our logic goes something like this: He was God, after all, and we are just human. So many times I have heard in church circles the statement "well, we are only human," usually when something goes wrong or when something needs a miracle or someone has slipped up! But Christ is in us the hope of glory. We have been given fullness in Him and we share in the divine nature. We are far from 'just human'. We are new creations, not improved versions of the old us, not warmed-up souls with a ticket to heaven, but brand new creations breathed into by God. He created in us a new nature and birthed divinity in us.

The heavenly and earthly walked in one body two thousand years ago. Jesus was a heaven and earth man. He was a prototype of the many sons and daughters who would come after Him because of resurrection. He was the first of a new breed; He was a model of us, not just a model for us.

We are encouraged to have the same mindset as Christ.

In your relationships with one another, have the same mindset as Christ Jesus: who, being in very nature God, did not consider equality with God something to be used to his own advantage... Philippians 2:5-6 (NIV)

Part of that mindset was that He knew his very nature. He knew He was God. I would like to propose to you that His powerful humility, His powerful sacrifice, which the rest of Philippians 2 talks about, was rooted in His powerful sense of significant identity. He was such a great servant because He was primarily a great son.

His sonship was applicable to his whole identity. As a man He was 100% a son, as God He was 100% the Son of God. He served as a mighty son, and we are to align our thoughts with His.

We are not "the Son of God," but we are sons of God. We have to allow our beliefs about our identity to track who we have become in Christ and not stay stuck in pre-resurrection, pre-conversion realities. We are to live in the new nature, which is truly Godlike – and put on the new nature (the regenerate self) created in God's image, [Godlike] in true righteousness and holiness (Ephesians 4:24, AMP)

Immerse yourself fully into this God-shaped new man from above! You are created in the image and likeness of God. This is what righteousness and true holiness are all about (Ephesians 4:24 MSG).

So what I am saying is we are called to have a high view of the new us. We are now the light of the world, we have authority to dispense forgiveness, we are glorious and we are being transformed into greater glory (Philippians 3:15; Matthew 5:14; John 20:23; 2 Corinthians 3:18).

In fact, in the rebuke I experienced in the kitchen, I sensed that His displeasure with the way I spoke about myself wasn't just about who I had become when I got saved, but who He had created from before the foundation of the earth.

2.4 I Am a Grand Design

I was praying one day, and I took a risk: I asked God what He thought of me. He said in that unmistakable inner audible voice, "I think you're beautiful." At this point I started to cry, and also worried that it didn't sound very masculine. In fact I told some friends that God had said I was beautiful and they thought I was being a bit girly too. So I had to journey through my and others' sexual stereotypes and begin to realise that God looks at me and thinks I am a thing of beauty. He doesn't do ugly. Something He would make always has the imprint of heaven's aesthetic; it's good and it's beautiful. It's also His opinion, and not a human one. He's not affected by stylised airbrushed models; He made real people like me and you. His voice and design is the standard, and by the heavenly standard, you're beautiful! Don't believe the mirror, the magazines or the media, or any other voice.

Put simply, God likes us, He's attracted to us and greatly values us. The stain of sin in our lives did not make God stop loving us. He doesn't just love me because He has to. He doesn't love me because He is a benevolent all-powerful being and it's His job to love. He's not looking at me and seeing no intrinsic value or beauty in me, and yet loving me because He is just the almighty altruist. He does not love me as a project, where He has all the resources and I am really worthless and broken but He can clean me up and give me value and that makes Him the almighty do-gooder. He's not a heavenly poverty relief agency who feels good about another one restored by His wonderful self. I am loved because to Him I am loveable.

He's not loving me with an agenda, where He loves me more when I get fixed, or loves me in order to fix me. He's not relating to me to fix me. If I stay broken, I am loved. If I stay unchanged, I am loved. I am loved because to Him I am loveable. To Him I have value and beauty whatever sin and life has done to warp me. I may have become un-lovely but He has and always will see past that. He put the gold in me. I am loved because He made me loveable. Because He made me.

Only Human?

A little Bible study may help.

We are all His workmanship

For we are his workmanship, created in Christ Jesus for good works, which God prepared beforehand, that we should walk in them. Ephesians 2:10

"Workmanship" here is from a Greek word that means we are His masterpiece, His special work of art.

We are all His offspring

"In him we live and move and have our being," as even some of your own poets have said, "For we are indeed his offspring." Being then God's offspring, we ought not to think that the divine being is like gold or silver or stone, an image formed by the art and imagination of man. Acts 17:28-29

The entire population of the earth is God's offspring.

What I am saying is that as long as an heir is under age, he is no different from a slave, although he owns the whole estate. The heir is subject to guardians and trustees until the time set by his father. So also, when we were under age, we were in slavery under the elemental spiritual forces of the world. But when the set time had fully come, God sent his Son, born of a woman, born under the law, to redeem those under the law, that we might receive adoption to sonship. Because you are his sons, God sent the Spirit of his Son into our hearts, the Spirit who calls out, "Abba, Father." So you are no longer a slave, but God's child;

and since you are his child, God has made you also an heir. Galatians 4:1-7

In this passage we can see the fact of our adoption as sons, but miss the scene painted in verses 1 to 3, where God is still seen as our father and we as His children, but we are "under age" and "under elemental forces." We were kids who were in slavery and who needed adopting. But there is no doubting all are His children before we were adopted. We were heirs but didn't know it.

God made man in His own image. And He made us good. And then it went horribly wrong. But make no mistake: we are lost treasure, lost sheep, and special coins. What got lost had unspeakable value to the Father and He seeks us with a passion and celebrates us with the angels (Luke 15:3-10).

He formed and knows us as individuals

For you formed my inward parts;
  you knitted me together in my mother's womb.
I praise you, for I am fearfully and wonderfully made.
Wonderful are your works;
  my soul knows it very well.
My frame was not hidden from you,
when I was being made in secret,
  intricately woven in the depths of the earth.
Your eyes saw my unformed substance;
in your book were written, every one of them,
  the days that were formed for me,
  when as yet there was none of them.
How precious to me are your thoughts, O God!
  How vast is the sum of them! Psalm 139:13-17

Only Human?

This passage is full of before-conception references, before-my-existence references – "made in secret"; "intricately woven in the depths of the earth"; "you saw my unformed substance"; "my days written in your book before there was one of them."

> ...even as he chose us in him before the foundation of the world, that we should be holy and blameless before him. In love he predestined us for adoption as sons through Jesus Christ, according to the purpose of his will... Ephesians 1:4-5

I believe these scriptures are telling us we were all pre-known, pre-loved and formed in God's thinking before creation itself. He didn't 'like' what we became at the fall, where Adam and Eve made bad choices and got expelled from Eden, creating a huge disaster for creation. But He loves who He originally designed us to be. And He is exerting his considerable resources and massive passion to restore each one to his or her original design, to what He originally thought and therefore still thinks.

He knows what He made us all to be originally. He loves that and is calling and drawing us into our original destiny, shaving off other opinions of our worth and usefulness, redeeming us from sin's power and penalty and stain; relieving us of our disappointments and self-curses in order to stand before Him and all creation as He originally intended us to be.

He loves you because He made you and He made you good and He made you unique and He made you significant and He made you beautiful.

Yes, before we trusted Jesus we were objects of wrath, at enmity, but God's love overcame our rejection of Him and called us back to Himself and to our original design (Ephesians 2:1-10).

So now I have to watch what I say about this awesome piece of cosmic design called "me." He doesn't want me to curse what He has made and blessed. He doesn't want me to dishonour with my words what He created. I am His grand design, you are His grand design, no exceptions, no exclusions.

This means we can prophesy original destiny over unbelievers, connect them to the original plan still ticking away inside them. It may be weak, perhaps as just a hidden wish or dream. But there is a trace of the original, the Father's fingerprints, something of heaven's design to be stirred.

We can heal the sick, literally restoring people's bodies to the original design and plan, before sin and life infected and broke them.

We can introduce heaven's wisdom into the marketplace, for everyone longs to be who they were made to be. The deeper wiring, the deeper reality is that they are His and His kingdom values resonate deeply with that DNA. He made us, so His stuff works. Heaven can invade the marketplace with success, without everyone needing to become Christians. Heaven's wisdom, strategies and values have resonance with all.

How we view the non-Christian world affects how we interact with it. I believe it's time to treat everyone with dignity as sons and heirs. Lost they may be, but they carry the maker's design and are objects of His eternal affection; it's time to believe that the Kingdom of Heaven works for everyone.

I am a grand design. They are His grand design. You are His grand design.

2.5 In Family Trinity

I was driving my car down the M8 motorway, and *we* (there's no one else in the car that I can see at this point) were just leaving Glasgow. I had my current favourite worship album on and my favourite track started to play. I was nodding my head to the beat and said out loud, "I really like this one, God." Instantly I could see Father, Son and Holy Spirit sitting in the car, and They were "rocking out" way more vigorously than I was to this tune and They said to me in one voice, "Yeah, we do too!" I was having a praise party in the car with the Trinity! I have since experienced being totally drunk in the Holy Spirit and driving the car quite safely. Health and safety legislation does not need to be changed to account for divine in-car encounters. I do keep my eyes open though.

I was getting an experiential revelation of the things I had begun to see in John 14. I am part of and wrapped up in family Trinity. They treat me as a fully paid-up member! John 14:18-20 says:

I will not leave you as orphans; I will come to you. Before long, the world will not see me any more, but you will see me. Because I live, you also will live. On that day you will realise that I am in my Father, and you are in me, and I am in you.

And verse 23:

Jesus answered him, "If anyone loves me, he will keep my word, and my Father will love him, and we will come to him and make our home with him."

So the Trinity is in me and I am in Them and They have come to make Their home with me. This is pretty exciting, and seems to be Jesus' normal expectation for the experience of all believers. Verse 20 says we will know or **realise** these facts, not just know about them. Extraordinary!

This is top-table dining, first-class travel, 5-star

accommodation on steroids. Talk about being rightly connected to royalty; I'm in Their family. You can't get any higher status than this. Being kings and queens with the King. If I had been born in Buckingham Palace and was first in line for the throne I would not be more exalted than this.

A few years ago, in a vision, I was walked past a long line of my spiritual heroes. I was being escorted by an angel to the very front of this queue. It was clear once I got to the front that it was for a very special audience with Father God, and I had pushed in...with angelic help! But the Father was talking right over my head, and I don't mean I couldn't understand because it was too weird or theological, but He was talking to someone much taller than me. Then I immediately found myself inside one leg of a large suit of armour and the angel said "This is yours." I also saw a very large sword floating in the air above me, at about the right height for someone who could actually wear the suit of armour.

I could sense I was being addressed as someone I couldn't associate with in terms of my size and stature. The angel said I could grow into the armour by declaring truth about my true identity. I realised I needed to line up with His opinion of me. He had obviously given me authority and significance beyond what I had considered to that point.

So I declared, and grew. The outcome was that I discovered the Father wanted face-to-face conversation with me. He didn't want me to grovel, but to grow into my true stature in Him, and He didn't want to come down to my level, He wanted to elevate me to His. He didn't want His greatness to make me feel insignificant. He wanted a father-son conversation, not a lord-to-minion or boss-to-underling relationship. His design for intimacy was as family members, and not as master to servants and slaves.

You see, Jesus took on the form of a servant, and became a sacrifice for us to elevate us with Him in His resurrection.

It is true that He gained for us more than Adam lost. We are exalted to a place of intimacy and privilege, of face-to-face encounter.

I needed help with this and still do. This level of relationship is so outside of any earthly concept, and certainly not a religious idea. Religion wants people to feel less significant, not totally liberated and empowered. We need the Holy Spirit; we need visions and supernatural encounters to help us. When Jesus said He left the Holy Spirit to be our guide, most of us assume (rightly) that is to steer us in life, but there is more. We also need a lot of Holy Spirit help to navigate the realms of heaven we are now privy to, and show us the reality of functioning as a new creation and all that is at our disposal. We need Him to show us the connection to the Father we now have.

I get to walk with the Father in the cool of the day again. He is present in my reality, but I am also present in His. In a way that was never true for Adam, He is sharing His reality with me and the new Eden is heaven and the walk is with Him in the cool of heavenly light.

We can't always fellowship in the burning intensity of full throne room glory, but there are many rooms in heaven, places to meet the Father in intimate conversation, or just be together, with no conversation needed.

Our sense of identity radically affects our intimacy.

2.6 Sat in the Right Place

To be seated with Christ in the heavenly realms is much more than a theological idea. It's not simply a spiritual reality that's true, but that we can't expect to experience, or that has little or no effect on everyday life. It's a reality that we have to adjust to and can access right now. We are so used to living on earth and looking to heaven from earth that we can think that all that happened was heaven invaded us – when it is also true that we were given a permanent position in heaven itself, from where we now live. This means we have both influence and authority. We have influence with our Father, who has invited us to speak to Him and make requests and share our desires. We have authority over the other spiritual realms because we are with Christ, and so above all other spirit rulers and authorities, which is why demons tremble in our presence and angels serve us.

He continues to invite me to pray more "from heaven" with the perspective and faith of an implementer of the realities I am seated in, my new norms. I believe this is why we never see Jesus "pray for the sick." He never asks, he just commands and declares "be healed"; "Lazarus, come forth." I am learning to command.

A young woman came forward for prayer on a Sunday morning in our church. She was responding to a word of knowledge about dyslexia. We prayed for her, and she asked if we could pray for her leg because she was a professional ballet dancer and one leg was shorter than the other. I thought, "Okay, we've seen a few legs grow and it's usually a straightening of a spine or re-aligning of hips." On questioning her she said it was none of these, but a lack of leg, of only about 1 centimetre, but enough for her to need a built-up ballet shoe to compensate. Internally I was now getting nervous, because I was realising I needed faith for more leg, not just a realignment. So I commanded this leg to grow a few times. Nothing happened immediately, so I did it again and she felt a burning sensation in her thigh and the leg grew. She no longer dances with a built-up shoe. There was extra bone, nerve and tissue created in those moments. (A couple of our ladies got hold of her afterwards and led her to Jesus and prayed for her to get baptised in the Spirit, so she got healed, saved and filled within thirty minutes.) When she went back to work her choreographer instantly noticed the change in her posture and how she danced. We have seen numbers get healed from hearing problems, back problems and all kinds of sickness and disease by commanding.

2.7 I Can Be Who I Was Born To Be

Someone said that I would really have got in touch with who I am in Christ when I genuinely wake up each morning and say "Father God, how am I going to change the world around me today?"

God's original design of you and your destiny are a perfect fit. No chafing. His plan isn't like tight-fitting jeans you can't button up or shoes that are too small. If what you feel you are called to is not resonating with who you are, then either you need more information from heaven, or you need to get in better touch with your true identity.

Life and upbringing can skew our view and affect our desires to the point that God's design feels awkward. We also have to remember that His design factors in our new creation, that Jesus now lives in us. So it will be filled with apparent impossibilities.

God has a vision for my life, a shape He calls into being. He gives scripture and prophetic words that paint the picture of who I am and what I can become in Him, my destiny and purpose. He sees into my future in Him and comes to me now with words of destiny to set the tracks of expectation to lead me to become all He intended.

Never is this a purpose that will jar with the aspirations of my renewed heart. We are each made for some unique and powerful purpose. The nearer I get to my fulfilled call, the more a giant thrill goes through me, one that turns all past trials into what they should be, momentary troubles on the way to His glorious purpose.

However, to be totally free to be who I am requires more than freedom from stuff. What I mean is it's not enough to be out of prison with no guards or fences – free from sin and its power, free from the law and free from Satan. That's like a criminal, set free, standing outside the prison gates in a new suit of clothes and a clean record, but only bus fare in his pocket. He pretty soon will end up back in jail! Real freedom includes freedom from things, but essentially includes freedom to do things, freedom to express who I am and move forward in my identity. Freedom means options that are genuine. Freedom means it's genuinely possible for the criminal to become Prime Minister, a plumber or a postman. All the resources need to be accessible for him to enter his destiny. Otherwise all he can do is take maybe one or two steps away from his past.

Lots of us end up "back in jail," because all we have been told is we are free from stuff. We celebrate freedom from sin, freedom from legalism and the power of Satan. We sing our freedom songs and dance outside the prison gate. We may even blow the odd raspberry at the guard on the wall. But we know we are called to something better, even something great. We know we have new clothes of righteousness, but the bus fare won't get us to be Prime Minister or even on a plumbing course. So we "do a few jobs" (behave like we used to) to keep ourselves going and soon we get entangled again. Then we need God to set us free again and around it can go.

My Heavenly Father gave me stuff, lots of great stuff. He hasn't just released me, He hasn't just designed me, He has resourced me. He's put the equivalent of a great wodge of cash in my account and arranged the appropriate training for my destiny.

My destiny is provided for by the Father who created it.

All the resources of heaven are available to this ex-convict. So world-changing days are now on the cards!

Only Human?

<u>Becoming What We Behold</u>

Second Kings 17 says *"They followed worthless idols and themselves became worthless."* Is the worthlessness many Christians feel rooted in their view of God? What you follow and worship affects your value – worth has its roots in what you see of God, how you see Him. You reflect the one you behold. Worshipping a god who thinks little of you produces smallness in you. In this passage they were worshipping gods who were blocks of wood or pieces of metal, unable to see and unable to save. Many of us have been told He doesn't do the miraculous anymore. A god who doesn't intervene, by implication, doesn't care. Jesus often moved miraculously out of compassion. As we follow and worship a compassionate and powerful God, the God of miracles, we will become like Him. It is totally incongruous to think that the worship of a powerful God who loves us produces a powerless people with a low view of their potential and significance.

My gifts, origins, position, family connections and the objects of my devotion create "me."

Like a recipe these ingredients make one whole, and when in good order, one wholesome cake. Like a composite material, these elements combine to create strength of identity, people who have a powerful "inner core."

Sometimes I've encountered the idea that Christianity is a constant mining out of the rubbish. The deeper we go the more rubbish we find, and so we are constantly discovering the depth of our depravity and brokenness. Peeling back the layers to reveal another area to be changed. I think that's such a shame; in fact it's missing something powerful, the spectacular effect of the death and resurrection of Jesus. Sure, there is rubbish to remove as we become more like Jesus; but its removal is to reveal a profound reality. It's to increasingly reveal the glory within and unveil the fantastic creative masterpiece that is you.

Someone once said that if you don't know who you are you will answer to any name, and if you don't know your assignment you will volunteer for any task.

You were designed for His presence.

2.8 The Enemy's Prime Target Revealed

In two key passages of scripture, our enemy's tactics are clearly revealed. Both Adam and Jesus represented humanity, Jesus as the last Adam. In Genesis and the Gospels, we see the devil tempting both Adam and Eve and Jesus.

Much has been made of his attempts to undermine God's word to Adam and Eve, and the test of obedience posed in the garden of Eden, and this is all valid. But what was his angle of attack? What was his target? Below we will see he was and is relentless in his attempts to subvert identity, seeking to create beliefs in his targets that cause them to accept they are less than they already are. And he is still pursuing the same strategy in every believer.

> *For God knows that when you eat of it your eyes will be opened, and **you will be like God**, knowing good and evil.* Genesis 3:15

Adam and Eve were tempted to act in order to change their identity, to improve, to be Godlike. To do this they had to first forget their true identity.

> *So God created man in his own image, in the image of God he created him; male and female he created them.* Genesis 1:27

It couldn't be clearer that they already were like God. In responding to the temptation to gain an identity already theirs, they actually lost out!

When Jesus had been fasting for forty days and He was hungry, Satan came to tempt Him.

> Then Jesus was led by the Spirit into the wilderness to be tempted by the devil. After fasting for forty days and forty nights, he was hungry. The tempter came to him and said, "<u>If you are the Son of God</u>, tell these stones to become bread."
>
> Jesus answered, "It is written: 'Man shall not live on bread alone, but on every word that comes from the mouth of God.'"
>
> Then the devil took him to the holy city and set him on the highest point of the temple. "<u>If you are the Son of God</u>," he said, "throw yourself down. For it is written:
>
> "'He will command his angels concerning you, and they will lift you up in their hands, so that you will not strike your foot against a stone.'" Jesus answered him, "It is also written: 'Do not put the Lord your God to the test.'"
>
> Again, the devil took him to a very high mountain and showed him all the kingdoms of the world and their splendour. "All this I will give you," he said, "if you will bow down and worship me."
>
> Jesus said to him, "Away from me, Satan! For it is written: 'Worship the Lord your God, and serve him only.'"
>
> Then the devil left him, and angels came and attended him. Matthew 4:5-11

The first two temptations are direct attacks on who He believed He was; "if you are the son of God." Jesus didn't need to do anything to prove to Himself or the devil who He was, He wasn't about to make Adam and Eve's mistake. In the third temptation He would have to forget who He was and what He had access to as the Son of God to fall for the "worship me" idea. He was God, the one who truly deserves all worship.

For Adam and Eve, trying to gain what they already had caused them to lose most of what they had! For in that moment they submitted to the one they believed. They began to serve and perform for "the prince of the power of the air," no longer fully representing God but becoming "sons of disobedience."

The Devil introduced a work, an action for them to do to become who they already were, and he's been doing that ever since. He's introduced "do more to be who you should be" into Christian thinking and culture. The fruit is striving, shame about who we are and performance. The performance can feel like it's for God because it's for a noble end, to be like Him. But actually we are jumping through hoops for the devil. This leads to a performance-based religion in which the devil is calling the tune.

> *You foolish Galatians! Who has bewitched you? Before your very eyes Jesus Christ was clearly portrayed as crucified. I would like to learn just one thing from you: did you receive the Spirit by the works of the law, or by believing what you heard? Are you so foolish? After beginning by means of the Spirit, are you now trying to finish by means of the flesh?* Galatians 3:1-3

The Christians in the region of Galatia were being told that to improve their Christianity they need to add the Old Testament law to their behaviour, especially circumcision; that they needed to add the rules to be more authentically godly. Paul's rebuke is swingeing; he says that in resorting to the realm of flesh – which includes human effort, and in the New Testament is the realm consistently in opposition to the

Spirit – they are placing themselves under a spell, literally a demonic "hex."

Later he tells them such behaviour is causing them to be alienated from Christ and to fall away from grace (Galatians 5:4).

He's saying that this religious performance, adding a thing to do to become something better, is obeying Satan and is deluding them and weakening them spiritually. They are **performing for Satan, not God.**

Who would have thought that performing could be disobedience!

We become world-changing believers not by working harder, but by believing who we really are, by standing in our true, powerful identity, by deepening our agreement with and submission to the reality that Christ is in us and we are in Him.

Religion has its roots in false identity, which is why religion is ultimately powerless. Religion is form – the external activities and procedures – without deep connection to God, who is the source of power. Religion is a realm of thought and activity fathered by the father of lies. He has "given birth" to a whole family of ideas and concepts, using Bible verses in many cases. These systems of thought, this family of lies, looks true, but is killing many believers on the inside. You don't have to sign up to the whole package to be affected; the seeds of religion are like leaven that affect the whole of your perspective through embracing small amounts.

Make no mistake; our enemy is adept at killing us through lies disguised as truth and scripture delivered in the wrong spirit. The devil will use scripture to try and kill you off. Look at the example of Jesus' temptation above. The devil quotes Psalm 91 accurately and says "just throw yourself off!" He's using well-quoted verses to try and kill the Messiah. The Bible in his mouth is murder.

If I am working hard at my faith but slowly dying on the inside, it's possible I am believing a lie about who I am. If I am burning out or killing my marriage in the name of Christianity it's possible I am performing for the wrong team. If I don't believe I can do what Jesus did because it's "just not me," or "I couldn't presume to be like Him," I am believing less of myself than God does. If I don't believe I am worthy of intimacy with the Father, or wonderful fullness of the Spirit, it's possible I am believing a fat lie. If I don't believe I am worthy of all God's blessings, it's possible I see myself as a lesser person than He does (Ephesians 1:3). If I believe just a bit more work will do it, I have bought a lie and I am living to gain identity I already have.

All of our efforts are springing from a good place, a heart to please God and a passion for His purpose; however, a few drops of religious thinking can produce real death by using our pure passions to fuel dead works.

The father of religion is Satan. And religion is death to our souls.

2.9 Sons or Servants?

The orphan identity and associated behaviour has its roots in the lack of experience of the presence of parents, not the lack of biological parents themselves. The lack of time in the presence of parents, with all that entails, produces orphanhood.

We are not left as orphans. The Father's plan was to continually saturate us with His presence to create a sonship identity, not simply to inform us that our adoption is complete and declared in the courts of heaven. To have legal adoption without the experienced activity of the new parent is, in the child's experience, to continue in the same state as before. A legal change without an experiential one is of little practical effect in the present experience of the child. He may get a different inheritance later, but that's it.

I will not leave you as orphans, I will come to you (John 14:18). He's the initiator and seeker, coming to continually saturate us with His powerful loving presence.

God came to Adam to walk with him. While men were building towers to reach to heaven, God came to Abraham to bless him. God came to Jacob, lying on a stone pillow, and showed him his presence, pulled back the curtain. God came to us in Jesus and Jesus sent the Spirit to us, so that His tangible presence and knowable voice could always be ours, that we would never walk as orphans or feel alone. We are not meant to simply claim the promise that He is with us, we are meant to daily walk in the experience of His presence. We are designed for it.

Orphans do not lack biological parents; they lack their presence.

I grew up as a Christian believing the ultimate goal was to be a faithful servant. Possibly the greatest source of my personal condemnation was the thought that I could be serving better or harder; I could be sacrificing more, and if I did go the extra mile, more pleasure would come to me from the Father and more breakthrough would come on the earth. I believed that my lack of power or fruit in any area was connected primarily to my lack of dedication.

My basic belief about my identity in Christ was that I was a servant of God, and that I was an average one at best.

This belief came from some great biblical sources. The apostle Paul regularly refers to himself and his co-workers as servants of Christ (Romans 1:1; Galatians 1:10; Colossians 4:12). First Corinthians 6:19-20 tells me that my body is a temple of the Holy Spirit, and that I am not my own; I was bought at a price.

To further strengthen the argument, the Greek word *doulos,* mostly translated "servant," is probably better translated "slave." Paul is saying he is a slave of Christ. He has laid his life down in every sense for the One who loves him.

How does this square with the scriptures:

> **For you did not receive the spirit of slavery** to fall back into fear, but you have received the Spirit of adoption as sons, by whom we cry, "Abba! Father!" The Spirit himself bears witness with our spirit that we are children of God... Romans 8:15
>
> You are my friends if you do what I command. **I no longer call you servants**, because a servant does not know his master's business. Instead, I **have called you friends**, for everything that I learned from my Father I have made known to you. You did not choose me, but I chose you and appointed you so that you might go and bear fruit – fruit that will last – and so that whatever you ask in my name the Father will give you. This is my command: love each other. John 15:14-17
>
> It is for **freedom** that Christ has set us free. Stand firm, then, and do not let yourselves be burdened again by a **yoke of slavery**. Galatians 5:1

Are we slaves or friends, free or bound, sons or servants? Often the answer is found in the tension, not in simply removing one side or the other. It is possible to be a son and a servant, just as Jesus was. Secure as a son, He served. The majestic truth is the Son came as a servant whilst losing none of His royal status, and so it is with us.

2.10 Free from Everything

Through His death and resurrection Jesus has freed us from every yoke, every possible force or influence that would control our life. We are truly free in every way. We are as free as He was.

We are free from spiritual death, we have passed from death to life (John 5:24; Colossians 2:13)
We are:

Free from self-pleasing (2 Corinthians 5:15)

Free from people-pleasing (Galatians 1:10; 1 Corinthians 7:23)

Free from the power of sin (John 8:34-36; Romans 6:14-23)

Free from bondage to the Law (Romans 7:6; Galatians 2:16; Galatians 3:10-13; Romans 10:4)

Free from the fear of physical death (Hebrews 2:14-15)

Free from the power of Satan and his elemental spiritual forces (Galatians 4:3-9; Colossians 2:8; Colossians 2:20)

This freedom puts us in a place where we get to choose. Choose to serve, choose to become "slaves of righteousness."

You, my brothers and sisters, were called to be free. But do not use your freedom to indulge the flesh; rather, serve one another humbly in love. Galatians 5:13

What then? Shall we sin because we are not under the law but under grace? By no means! Don't you know that when you offer yourselves to someone as obedient slaves, you are slaves of the one you obey –

whether you are slaves to sin, which leads to death, or to obedience, which leads to righteousness? But thanks be to God that, though you used to be slaves to sin, you have come to obey from your heart the pattern of teaching that has now claimed your allegiance. You have been set free from sin and have become slaves to righteousness. Romans 6:15-18

We are in the most powerful place possible, able to choose to be obedient from the heart. To choose as sons to also serve, to choose as friends to please our Friend with our worship.

Jesus is our model. He knew who He was, He was God, yet He took on Himself the form of a servant (Philippians 2:6-7). He was clear in His identity as God's Son and was able to "volunteer" to take on the servant identity without ever relinquishing his fundamental nature as God. In John 13:3-4 we see it clearly expressed:

Jesus knew that the Father had put all things under his power, and that he had come from God and was returning to God; so he got up from the meal, took off his outer clothing, and wrapped a towel round his waist.

He knew who he was, where He was from, where He was going and He served them.

As the most free and powerful person that ever lived, Jesus served humanity, laying down His life. In His last hours none of His power or status was diminished. He could have called twelve legions of angels, and they would have come. He released forgiveness to the thief on the cross next to Him.

We are sons and daughters of the Most High God, royalty, children of the King. And He calls us friends, He reveals to us mysteries, He reveals to us His plans and perspectives. We have all the rights and privileges of sons (John 1:12; Romans 8:17). From that powerful place of privilege, we gladly take on the role of servants of the Most High. You need to be powerful to lay down your life.

2.11 Comfortable with the Uncomfortable

Jesus said a lot of things that were challenging, even hard to understand, and therefore uncomfortable. One day He was teaching and started to talk about it being important that people "eat His flesh and drink His blood." That could be a title for a zombie-meets-vampire movie! But it's actually scripture.

The words about eating flesh and drinking blood were hard to hear, but those listening could detect something beyond sense…Life.

The words of God in the hands of the Spirit of God are true and freeing and life-imparting. He is not just the way and the truth!

Believing God's declarations, opinions and pronouncements about me is vital. He doesn't pronounce things based on my circumstances or even good sense from a human point of view. Don't look for proof in your history or circumstances.

The enemy has duped many into thinking what is comfortable is true. Comfortable is usually linked to familiar and what has become our normal. I find people aren't always comfortable with God's definition of their identity. It comes from heaven; its perspective is different. It's supernatural by nature. Our initial inner comfort is not the best test. The witness of the Spirit and Word are our test. Let's not take our readings about ourselves from our flesh, fuelled by our natural reasoning. Let's diligently push through our discomfort to come to the place where our opinions agree with His.

The Spirit gives life; the flesh counts for nothing. The words I have spoken to you – they are full of the Spirit and life. John 6:63

He has the words of eternal life, and that includes His definition of you. His words are always life-giving and hope-producing; now that's heaven's style of comforting!

PART 3

INTIMACY AND ENCOUNTER

A few years ago I sent this email to one of our leaders:

Hi Jan

Here's a quick summary:

Personally I have been having amazing times with God and He is speaking to me and beginning to give me a greater level of revelatory encounter with Himself. These are not about things or people, just seeing more of Him. (See Psalm 63:2; Psalm 17:15; Psalm 41:12; Psalm 61:7; Ephesians 1:15-18; Hebrews 4:16) I believe we have underestimated what it is to come before the throne of grace; that David had repeated revelatory encounters with God's form, face, glory and power. And this is available to us all in the new covenant (2 Corinthians 3:18 says we all reflect or 'contemplate' the Lord's glory by the Spirit). It is definitely linked to not striving. This is entry by grace and faith, not pushing and qualifying.

In this section we explore what this looks like and how we can become more aware of heaven's realm.

3.1 Struck Dumb in Prayer

It was a strange experience. For over three months, I literally couldn't ask God for anything in prayer. Nothing would come out of me – I was struck dumb in prayer! All I could do was worship and linger in His presence. I was like Zechariah in Luke 1:19-20. He was struck dumb when an angel told him he was going to have a child and he didn't believe it.

With hindsight He was retraining me, leading me to a place of faith-filled praying. He wanted me to speak about things in His presence with a heart of faith. He was also recalibrating my desires, what was primary, what was drawing me to Him.

At the end of this period He said, "Okay, it's time to ask," and He reminded me of the many promises where we are to ask and receive that our joy may be full. What tumbled out of me was, "God, the only thing I want is You." It wasn't calculated or rehearsed, it was instinctive. My inner orientation had changed. My "blank cheque" moment in His presence had passed, and I just wanted Him. Intimacy had become my highest desire, a desire above success, provision, healing, great ministry, healthy family – *I just want You, Jesus*, was the cry of my heart.

He has moved heaven and earth to renew intimacy with His highest creation. He likes us and He wants to spend time with us for its own sake.

I had underestimated what it means to come freely to the Throne of Grace. I started to read the Psalm with **new** eyes. It's clear David was having revelatory experiences of the presence of God on a regular basis. Perhaps he understood his access better than I had done. The Psalm depict a man that is so in love with the Presence that it's his main thing in life. With a nation to run and wars to fight, the one thing he is seeking after, his single-hearted pursuit, was to gaze on the beauty of the Lord, to gaze upon His power and glory, seeing His face every day (Psalm 27:4; Psalm 63:2; Psalm 17:15). In some unspecified way David was seeing God and His glory; these weren't theories to him. He knew His nature because he was seeing it, tasting it, experiencing it and then writing down what that was like. He wrote of rivers of delights, of endless joy in His presence. This wasn't Theology in the sense that he was writing what was true because someone had told him it was true, this was inspired writing flowing directly from personal experience. He was creating good theology from his encounters.

I started to believe I could see as David saw. I would worship and increasingly expect to see something. And I was frequently led on visionary encounters played out in my imagination. Sometimes things happened that overlaid an image on my natural sight. The Holy Spirit was redeeming my mind and my imagination.

His images started to play out on the screen of my mind. I also felt Him physically; I was frequently shaking in my room where no one could see me. The hair on my arms would stand on end, laughter would come and sometimes tears. He was affecting my mind, my body and my emotions.

3.2 Beholding

Jesus prayed we would be where He is and behold His glory. This is an invitation to every believer right now, not some far-off dream, not just when we die.

> *Father, I desire that they also, whom you have given me, may be with me where I am, to see my glory that you have given me because you loved me before the foundation of the world.* John 17:24

Paul experienced such encounters, some of which empowered and equipped him for his ministry. He saw other things he couldn't speak about! (See Ephesians 3:3 & 7; 2 Corinthians 12:1-4.) Paul's teaching didn't come from study but from revelations and acts of God's power in his life. Visions and dreams are the natural outflow and consequence of the coming of the Holy Spirit on the believer (Acts 2:17). I believe every believer can have these kinds of encounters; they are not just for "special ones," or people with certain gifts.

The renewal of the mind extends beyond thinking Bible thoughts or possessing godly attitudes, to the complete surrender of the imagination to the Holy Spirit, allowing Him to be the projectionist onto the screens of our hearts and minds.

We should have no more problem with inviting the Holy Spirit into our minds than we do with inviting Jesus into our hearts.

> *If then you have been raised with Christ, seek the things that are above, where Christ is, seated at the right hand of God. Set your minds on things that are above, not on things that are on earth.* Colossians 3:1-2

Things that are above are heavenly things. We are seated with Him in heavenly realms so we can set our minds to gaze upon and be filled with heaven's realities.

Jesus lived a life of revelation. He only did what He saw the Father doing; He saw things in "heaven" while He was on earth. John 8:38 – "I am telling you what I have seen in the Father's presence." We get an insight into His times with the Father when He takes Peter, James and John up the mountain and is transfigured before them. Moses and Elijah show up and the Father comes in a cloud of His presence. This is the only recorded account of this happening, but this kind of encounter could have been more common for Jesus in His times with the Father. He did say to Nathaniel, *"Truly, truly, I say to you, you will see heaven opened, and the angels of God ascending and descending on the Son of Man,"* (John 1:51) expressing the kind of spiritual reality He was living in and which others would be able to see. In His discussion with Nicodemus He said, *"No one has ascended to heaven but He who came down from heaven, that is, the Son of Man who is in heaven"* (John 3:13 NKJV).

Jesus was not confused about His location. He was living in two dimensions or realms of existence at the same time and was seeing one whilst living in the other. Heaven's realities – angels and the Father's presence – were constantly interacting with Him. He was enjoying them and experiencing them. Angels came to Him at the end of His fast, and He was aware he could summon twelve legions of angels at His arrest in the garden of Gethsemane. Jesus was comfortable with these realities and interactions.

In Christ earth and heaven walked hand in hand in total communication. He walked as heaven on earth, He was the kingdom come. Then He took 'earth to heaven' in His resurrection. There is now a man in heaven, and we are seated there with Him. We have been raised to an exalted place, seated with Christ in heavenly realms whilst walking on the earth. We are learning to do what He demonstrated, learning the language and form of heaven's communication, and learning to explore heaven now.

The early church was utterly dependent on such heaven-to-earth interactions for its progress. Dreams, visions and angelic activity litter the book of Acts. Here's one example, when Peter was on the roof of a house: *"He fell into a trance.* **He saw** *heaven opened and something like a large sheet..."* (Acts 10:10-11). This resulted in a great breakthrough into the gentile world.

Heaven is our realm now, not just earth.

I've been going to the gym for close to seventeen years, trying to stay fit. Every now and again I need to change what I do. I need to attend a new class. This helps prevent boredom and also helps my muscles not to get used to the same programme and so dull its effect. Every time I change class I get nervous. There are new moves to learn, the instructors are different. I should be okay; I am a fully paid-up member, I have every right to be there, but somehow the first few weeks I feel a foreigner in my own gym. I think our position in Heaven is like this. We are fully paid-up members but we don't know the moves, it's a strange environment and we are completely unfamiliar and out of our comfort zone. We need the Holy Spirit, as teacher and guide, to help us navigate this new realm and get our new moves into our new normality. It's uncomfortable at first and can therefore feel "unnatural," but we were born for this. And just as a baby was born to walk, yet has to learn and sometimes fall, we were born for heavenly encounters, dreams and visions.

3.3 See God and Die?

I was told if I saw Him I would die. Is it true?

Jesus said the opposite in the Beatitudes:

Blessed are the pure in heart, for they shall see God.
Matthew 5:8

"Pure in heart" here means "unmixed or unalloyed." In classical Greek "pure" (*katharos*) described a river whose course was clear and open. Here it means singleness of heart and undivided devotion. In other words, the devoted ones shall continually behold God. The way has been made, that wasn't made before. We are beholding His glory and being changed as a result (2 Corinthians 3:18).

If Moses *"persevered because he **saw Him** who is invisible"* (Hebrews 11:27 NIV) how much more can we? This scripture is saying we are hugely happy (blessed) as we see God. The new covenant changed everything. The cross and resurrection changed everything.

There is a fullness of "seeing" to come, but that doesn't preclude awesome encounters and revelations of His face now. All encounters are transformational; it's impossible to behold Him and not become more like Him. The ultimate encounter illustrates this powerfully. When He appears He will transform us completely. When we see Him we will become like Him, for we will see Him as He truly is (1 John 3:2).

<u>The End of Distance</u>

Any notion of distance from God for the believer creates a problem. The gap has to be filled, it's a vacuum that needs solutions; and it gets filled with notions of payment, penance, works, effort, and religious observance.

We were distant, now we are not. We are reconciled; that means close. Enmity has gone, relationship and intimacy are restored (Romans 5:10; Colossians 1:21-22). We are one spirit with the Lord (1 Corinthians 6:19).

There are no limits to our exploration of Him. Our friendship with God has no boundaries. His knowing and longing for us is relentless too. The Spirit yearns inside us to connect deeper, to enjoy intimate friendship with us. All ideas of distance have been removed from God's mind; they need to disappear from ours too. Here's some scriptures that illustrate this reality –

Or do you suppose that the Scripture is speaking to no purpose that says, *"The Spirit Whom He has caused to dwell in us **yearns** over us and He **yearns** for the Spirit* *[to be welcome] with a jealous love?"* (James 4:5 AMP). *Righteousness by faith realised means unlimited friendship with God* (Romans 5:1 Mirror Word Translation).

Deism has afflicted our view of God. Deism says God is holy and mighty, He created everything, but then like a watchmaker He withdrew to a distance from the world as He let it function. If we lift up His greatness and awesome power, celebrate His holiness but never enjoy and celebrate our intimacy and union, we are in danger of creating a gap between us out of a false idea of true reverence.

The idea that only special people get close has its roots in the Old Testament. But the idea of an intermediary was initiated by the people, not God. God intended to invite all the people up Mount Sinai to meet with Him but they got scared and asked Moses to speak to God for them (Exodus 19:6 & 13; Exodus 20:19). He intended a nation of priests, but fear got in the way. The religious thinking and practice that were set up at this point, that preserved distance, were demolished by Jesus' teachings and actions.

He brought us close and He has come close. He loves our presence, He showers us with affection.

Peace with God is a place of unhindered enjoyment of friendship beyond guilt, suspicion, blame or inferiority.

3.4 Stepping into Encounters

There are many different ways we experience God. He impacts every dimension of our being. Here are some of the ways He impacts us.

<u>i) Inner encounters, or seeing with the heart</u>

> *I pray that the <u>eyes of your heart may be enlightened</u> in order that you may know the hope to which he has*

called you, the riches of his glorious inheritance in his holy people, and his incomparably great power for us who believe. Ephesians 1:18-19

David said that his soul thirsted for the Lord. That thirst is satisfied as God shines His light, pours in His love and reveals the glory of the face of Jesus inside us, powerfully and beautifully enlightening our inner reality with His presence. Encountering God puts love and fire and nourishment into our inner man (Romans 5:5; 2 Corinthians 4:6).

ii) Bodily encounters

Here's some scripture pointing to the effect of God on your body:

My body longs for you. Psalm 63:1

...as he spoke, the Spirit came into me and raised me to my feet. Ezekiel 2:1

*If I say, "I will not mention him, or speak any more in his name," there is in my heart as it were a burning **fire** shut up in my bones, and I am weary with holding it in, and I cannot.* Jeremiah 20:9

When Jesus said "I am he," they drew back and fell to the ground. John 18:6

The Holy Spirit coming on you or pouring out of you can make your body feel things and do things. God loves all of you – every dimension of your existence matters to Him. Physical experiences of Him are not more or less profound than unseen ones.

iii) Emotional encounters

By emotional encounters I mean the way God fills us and invades us so it has more than just an inner effect that is unseen. But our emotional state is affected. There are many biblical examples of this.

Early believers were intoxicated in the Spirit. We see in Acts 2:13-15 and Ephesians 5:18, that Holy Spirit activity on people has some outward parallels to drunken behaviour. At least that is what many onlookers thought of the observed behaviour in Acts 2.

King David called it "the river of delights" and being filled with "joy in your presence" (Psalm 36:8; Psalm 16:11). Often we have limited the sense of this to merely inner activity, something reflective and contained within. True joy overflows; it affects the countenance. You only really know if you are joyful if it affects others around you.

To relegate emotions to the place of suspicion or unimportance is yet another way we think that the "unseen" is more spiritual. To imagine a feelings-free relationship with a passionate, loving Heavenly Father has more to do with Plato than scripture. It's from that ancient Greek philosopher that we get the idea of 'Platonic' relationships. These are relationships free of emotional baggage. The mind is seen as superior, the intellect the higher faculty. This actually isn't Christianity but Greek philosophy. How did people know Jesus was anointed with joy? How does the Father feel about those He loves? He is moved by His compassion; He has a feeling, a surge of emotional energy that propels Him to action.

To be moved with compassion is not the description of someone thinking it through and coming to a logical outcome. Love, joy and compassion have their roots in emotion spilling out into expression. When you look at the original language of Zephaniah 3:17 you see God spinning around over His people under the influence of a strong emotion, you see God rejoicing, and shouting because He feels mighty things. We are made in His image and are designed to behave as He does!

God Encounters are Holistic

We have seen above how David's encounters affected his body so that it wanted more of God: his flesh cries out. He experienced joy in the river of delights. The prophets experienced physical sensations and movement when God was at work in them and on them. These things can all happen together. Joy is meant to flow out from an inner reality to an outward one. God's wrap-around presence affects us on every level, with different aspects emphasized at different times.

Being Open to Encounter

God is a person. God is also three people – Father, Son and Spirit. He is a relational being who lives in a vibrant pulsating reality of the spirit realm, heaven. In His presence is fullness of joy. He wants us to know Him as a person in a holistic, deep, experiential way alongside a growing mental knowledge. They belong together.

I don't want to be the guy who thinks it is thunder when it is the voice of the Lord (John 12). I don't want to be someone who can be in a place where God is strongly present and not be able to recognise it. I am about learning His ways, tuning to His wavelength and not missing the beauty and variety of the ways He reveals Himself experientially to us.

It's possible to be right next to God doing or saying something and miss it or misinterpret it. I want to trust how He works in me and on me and tune in to His normal, which may be quite unusual to me.

Encounters Require Trust

This is about giving Him control and complete access to every part of us, our heart, emotions, mind, will, body and soul, accepting all that God has for us and wants to do in us, however that comes and whatever that looks like.

That requires trust that Father God loves us and wants what is best for us; that He is safe, not precocious or punishing. Trust that He likes us and that He is in pursuit of us. It requires a voluntary yielding of control, a submission to His presence, which could be a feeling, a movement, a revelation in the ways we already discussed.

This is a **process**. As we trust and let go He frees us up; as He frees us up and heals us, we trust and let go. The more confident we get in His love the more our fears subside and we enjoy Him in His realm in His way. That's knowing God.

Luke 11 is an encouragement to this, to trust the good Father who wants to give more of His best gift, which is Himself, the Holy Spirit.

What father among you, if his son asks for a fish, will instead of a fish give him a serpent; or if he asks for an egg, will give him a scorpion? If you then, who are evil, know how to give good gifts to your children, how much more will the heavenly Father give the Holy Spirit to those who ask him! Luke 11:11-13

The Fruit of Intimate Encounter

Increased thirst for God

Revelatory experiences awaken in us a ravenous appetite for God and His presence. The more we have the more we want.

The exciting thing is that we all have the capacity to see,

drink, receive, encounter; this is not a special gift.

There is also no end to His capacity to delight and reveal, for there is no end to Him. We will spend eternity going "Wow, I hadn't seen that before!"

How lovely is your dwelling-place, O LORD Almighty! My soul yearns, even faints, for the courts of the LORD; my heart and my flesh cry out for the living God. Psalm 84:1-3

Increased impact for God

What goes on around us is according to what goes on inside us.

Bill Johnson says, "Each encounter works in our hearts, bringing about the needed transformation so that we might be entrusted with more of Him. The more profound the work of the Spirit is within us, the more profound the manifestation of the Spirit flowing through us."

We have increasing impact from a place of deepening intimacy and real relationship. It's where we learn and see what the Father is doing.

*Now to Him who is able to do far more abundantly beyond all that we ask or think, according to the power that works **within** us…* Ephesians 3:20

So Jesus said to them, "Truly, truly, I say to you, the Son can do nothing of his own accord, but only what he sees the Father doing. For whatever the Father does, that the Son does likewise. For the Father loves the Son and shows him all that he himself is doing. And greater works than these will he show him, so that you may marvel." John 5:19-20

Know the Word

In our thirst for intimacy and the truth of God, we can, and should, invest in a deepening knowledge of scripture.

The rather sobering truth is that the people who resisted Jesus the most were the ones who knew their scriptures the best. Their mission to the nations to find converts was not commended by Jesus.

The pursuit of theology (learning about God) can be mentally stimulating and rewarding, but that on its own doesn't produce intimacy; God is a person and wants relationship. We don't connect to concepts but to a being. Of course, great concepts can help us do that, but the knowledge without the experience is a road to pride and not encounter with Him. We can think we know Him because we have head knowledge, because we can rehearse the concept accurately, but we don't really know Him in the biblical sense of knowing by experience (*ginóskó*). It's not enough to be able to pass the test of biblical orthodoxy with correct concepts and scriptures.

So for example, coming with confidence before the Throne of Grace and entering the holy place, the full-on presence of God, as described in the passage in Hebrews quoted below:

> *Therefore, brothers and sisters, since we have confidence to enter the Most Holy Place by the blood of Jesus, by a new and living way opened for us through the curtain, that is, his body, and since we have a great priest over the house of God, let us draw near to God with a sincere heart and with the full assurance that faith brings, having our hearts sprinkled to cleanse us from a guilty conscience and having our bodies washed with pure water. Let us hold unswervingly to the hope we profess, for he who promised is faithful.* (Hebrews 10:19-23; see Hebrews 4:16)

Is a clear invitation to enter experientially into a throne room encounter with the Lord regularly. "We have confidence to enter," "let us draw near." The issue is not "knowing we can," or that "we will when we die and are with Him in heaven," but that we do. That every one of us has regular "throne room encounters" with the Lord of Glory that are experiences we can describe. I would suggest that what the passage shows us that is the issue of whether we do this or not is faith and not knowledge. If you believe you can, and this is for you, then you will. The cross has made you clean, so experiences of the throne room are yours right now.

The passage also shows us that this is a significant part of our hope; a present hope of experiencing the holy place. Renew your hope that the holy place is for you today! This is part of the hope of glory that we have because He is in us. It's the hope of encountering the glory of the one we love.

Why not take a moment, right now! This opportunity has already been established at the cross and resurrection and is for every believer. Don't just agree with the statement, experience the statement's realities. Also, don't "work up to it." This is not based on your works, but His completed work for you.

So let's not objectify God, making Him a thing we know about rather than a person we have real connection with. A "thing" can be relegated to a drawer, a library, or to heaven far, far away. The Person is always around you, always inside you, always inviting you into deeper experiences and infinite intimacy.

3.5 More Glory

Theresa and I took a short sabbatical at Bethel Church in Redding, California. While we were there we took a trip to the giant redwood trees on the coast. They are amazing.

We went for a forest walk and on returning to the car found something like gold dust or glitter all over the dashboard and windowsills in the front of the car. A while later we were back home in Scotland and we went for a walk up a mountain with our daughter and son-in-law. We had a good time but it was very wet and we were in cloud most of the time. We got back soaked and tired. The weather in Glasgow was brighter so we put our coats, trousers and boots outside to dry. We were startled to find our boots glistening with bright glitter. It was on our waterproof trousers and jackets. There it was, just sparkling in the sun. At first we thought we must have walked through mineral deposits; then we found it on other areas of our clothes. The clincher was when we found this glittery golden stuff inside our jackets! Maybe the cloud on the Munro had been, at least in part, a glory cloud?

Why would He do this? What does it mean? We were blessed and excited by God's extravagance in the way He showed us some of His glory. That's a good answer for me.

I was reading a book called *They Told Me Their Stories*. It is a book of first-hand accounts from the Azusa Street revival. It began in a converted stable in Azusa Street, Los Angeles, and ran for about three and a half years from 1906 to 1910. It provided the spark and initial force to the Pentecostal movement and subsequently the Charismatic movement. It is commonly known for the experience of Baptism in the Spirit, which included speaking in tongues. This was the first mass outbreak of this phenomenon since the early church, although there had been several forerunners.

You don't have to look very far to find much more going on at Azusa. These first-hand accounts are by folk who were teenagers at the time of the outpouring. They tell of the constant manifest glory of God that hung in the room like a shimmering cloud. You could part it with your fingers; you could hide in it in places, it was so thick. Then they tell of miracle after miracle of healing that took place in that atmosphere. All these youth were involved in praying for the sick and seeing cancers leave and many walk out of wheelchairs. Some of them were on "clean up squad" to sweep up tumours off the floor that had fallen off people as they got healed.

It strikes me that the New Covenant is a better covenant than the old, which came with glory. There was glory on the mountain top that Moses had to climb, and glory on Moses' face every time he met with God. There was glory manifested so thick in the new temple that the priests could not minister. This was all for a covenant that the apostle Paul now says is obsolete. He says the new covenant comes with greater glory and that we can behold it in increasing measure. Some commentators say it is the glory simply of the higher and more wonderful truth of the gospel of grace rather than the covenant of law. Now of course that is true, but 2 Corinthians 3 is also telling us that the two covenants both appeared in manifest glory, and that of the new exceeds and transcends the old, and we can see it and reflect it. Put another way, the revelation of the truths of the two covenants came with an accompanying manifestation of glory, and the new manifestation will greatly exceed the old.

This makes manifest presence so important. Intellectual acknowledgment is insufficient for human transformation; only encounters with God's glory in some form truly transform us. Be it in our bodies, hearts or minds, we need to encounter Him.

I believe we are seeing increasingly powerful manifestations of God's presence and it's changing people's lives. It's changing their view of God and what they think the Christian life is about. It is bringing new freedom into their hearts and clarity to their thinking, and putting fire inside them for Jesus. What we are seeing is the beginning. There is more.

Seeking His Presence is Our Number One Priority

Blessed are those who have learned to acclaim you, who walk in the light of your presence, Lord. Psalm 89

PART 4

IS HEAVEN ABOUT TO COLLAPSE?

What many Christians believe about the realm of healing is tantamount to having faith in the demise of heaven as a cohesive force in the universe.

We pull heaven back together in this chapter, and give the topic of healing a thorough examination!

4.1 A British Problem?

I have been praying for the sick for decades. You've heard some of my story and struggle earlier in the book. I have gone through times of breakthrough, great elation and deep discouragement. My conclusion is that in the West we have a number of problems that get in the way of us experiencing more in this area. What I have realised is that the challenge is on my end: I have struggled with deeply rooted perspectives and values inherited from my culture and some of my Christian forebears.

My problems were grouped around five categories, and in my experience I think they apply to many of us.

1) **Worldview.** We are "healing blind" and "supernatural blind" because we live in a sceptical western culture, where science has to explain everything and the miraculous has been dispensed with as antiquated.

You can read whole lumps of scripture and "not see" the miraculous content. One of our leaders admitted one day that he had been reading the Bible for years and had never seen how often angels were involved. He always substituted "God" or "Holy Spirit" or some other vague notion of what was involved, rather than see angels.

2) **Theology.** What is God's will? Where does suffering and our theology of death fit in a developed theology of healing? Many are confused about this and their biblical convictions, or lack thereof, are a major roadblock to faith.

3) **Experiential.** Disappointments and failure have accompanied many brave attempts to bring healing; the result is discouragement and deep questions. The reality is that success is also tough to handle well.

4) **Pastoral.** This is connected to point 3. We live in a very "pastoral" Christian culture. We don't want to get people's hopes up if we can't deliver. What do we say to very sick people who have had prayer and nothing has happened? How do we manage and help people who are near death? What do we say to their relatives? This emotional set of questions can push in right ahead of any faith for breakthrough. It gets in the way. Even though it's important to care for people, the most caring thing we can do is see them healed!

5) **American TV evangelists.** With apologies to my many American friends, the British definitely struggle with this. Style issues, moral failures of the past, culture crossover issues, and appeals for money are off-putting. It's a pity because some of them see amazing miracles and we just can't handle the packaging.

All of these issues, bar one, are tackled in more depth

elsewhere in this book. Here we want to focus on our biblical convictions.

If you are sick, there is healing for you as you read these pages. I pray God deepens your understanding and faith for healing miracles in your own body and for those you meet.

4.2 Let's Get All the Verses Together!

Healing is a challenging subject and the Old Testament throws us a few curveballs along the way. Yet it's inspired by God; it's essential narrative, God-breathed information. Paul tells us it has great value, because all scripture is inspired by God. But you have to rightly divide the word of truth. That means use it with care, insight and appropriate application.

The problem with a "let's get all the verses together on healing" approach to sorting out the Bible's teaching on it is that it ignores some other important elements of the way the Bible builds the narrative and teaches us about God.

In no way is the Bible a systematic book. It's not a reference guide to God. We often wish it was, and so we study it in the way I suggest above, believing every verse to have the same weight and bearing on the matter as another. We collect biblical data about God in a way he didn't intend. We can search for anything in seconds now and have lists of verses right there on our phones. However, He wrote us stories, poems, songs, prophecies and histories. It does have a structure and that is pointed to in the way we refer to our Bibles as Old and New Testaments or Covenants. Jesus made a New Covenant in His blood, and it replaced the Old. The Old Testament is a story of His covenants from Adam to David. It contains multiple covenants that build on each other and prepare us for the final one, made by Jesus.

Covenant

Simply put, a covenant is an unbreakable bond made in blood and sworn between two parties. It is stronger than a contract and more binding than most agreements we see in modern culture. It usually involves the killing of animals and spilling their blood. This is a sign of its value and seriousness. The parties swear that they will keep this agreement or die. Death was the consequence of broken covenants in most cases. In this dramatic way God binds Himself to man. In each covenant He describes the terms of the agreement, its boundaries and requirements. It is often accompanied by a sign. For Noah there was a rainbow; for Abraham there was circumcision. The sign is a reminder of the covenant made.

Here are the covenants that make up the Old Testament section of our Bibles:

Covenant with Adam – Hosea 6:7. This is referred to retrospectively by the prophet, but Adam and God had a relationship and it had one simple boundary with a life or death consequence: don't eat from that tree or you will die.

Covenant with Noah – Genesis 9:8-17. On the whole planet there was so much evil. It was the continued reflection and preoccupation of men's hearts. God found one honourable man. With him He made a covenant in which God pledged to never do the flood thing again, no matter how bad it got. God pledged patience, a holding back of what men may deserve. He was saying "I'm not going to step in again in a catastrophic way to stop evil's momentum." He also pledged a stable planet in which other covenants can unfold toward the ultimate end. His guaranteed forbearance is signified every time you see a rainbow.

Covenant with Abraham – Genesis 15:18. God promised Abraham a lot. Multiple descendants, nations coming from him, a land, multiplied blessing. He committed himself to fulfilling it; it was incredibly one-sided. God stood in the blood of the covenant and said He Himself would act to fulfil this for Abraham. It demonstrates the giving grace of God. It points to His ultimate commitment to humanity expressed at the cross.

Covenant with Israel – Exodus 24:8. Here we have Moses giving the law to a nation. Now there are extensive dos and don'ts. There was much shedding of blood. The people promised and God promised. Here God made a covenant with a nation rather than an individual, and it's the nation that He promised would come from Abraham.

Covenant with David – Psalm 89:3. David is king of the nation of Israel; God pledges to build him a house, a long-lasting dynasty. He promised that he would always have a king that was his offspring sat on Israel's throne. With this He sets up a lineage and pointer toward the King who was to come.

We know God is the same, He changes not. His nature is consistent (Hebrews 13:8, Malachi 3:6). But what's harder to see is that He changes the way we experience him according to the covenant we are in. So before Noah we had God wiping out the inhabitants of the earth. After His covenant with Noah, He says He won't do that again. No one since Noah has experienced that expression of God's nature. He is the same, but we have experienced different things from Him since that covenant came into force. They had a deluge. We have a rainbow.

Before Moses there weren't all the rules and regulations to keep, there was no tent and no fire at night and cloud by day.

Before David there was no singing and dancing before the Ark of the Covenant. Under the Mosaic regulations only one priest a year was allowed in before the Ark, and they used to put a rope round his leg in case the experience killed him. It meant they could drag him out without entering themselves. With David it was different (1 Chronicles 16). The free access to the presence of God in David's era was more akin to the New Covenant; it pointed forward, whilst directly contradicting the Mosaic covenantal rules in force at the time. People were experiencing God differently in David's day than in Moses' era.

It's not the purpose of this chapter to explain the full development of the covenants and how God fulfilled His end consistently. It's a good study though, and there are good sources for this. (For example, see *The Christ of the Covenants* by O. Palmer Robertson.)

The point is to see the changing way God revealed Himself to us through Old Testament history. God's consistency is present at a deeper level than is first apparent. He is a covenant-making and a covenant-keeping God (1 Kings 8:23). What was allowable behaviour before the Lord changed; some things that He said you couldn't do under Moses, David did and He was okay with it; in fact it was His idea (2 Chronicles 29:25). Gad the king's seer and Nathan the prophet commanded the change in worship approach. They spoke from God. You can see it as a contradiction, because Moses spoke from God, or you can see it as development, man's capacity to live with the presence of God increasing. He is always seeking to dwell with man and to be intimate with him.

There is an unfolding from heaven, a developing revelation of God which meant things were replaced and renewed. The biggest shift of all was Jesus, and He really got in trouble for it. He didn't just challenge their interpretation of Mosaic law, He authoritatively rewrote chunks of it!

4.3 Jesus Rewrote the Rules

Jesus introduced a new era and consummated it at the cross. Here's a list of things He changed. It's not exhaustive, but it illustrates the point.

1) Matthew 5:38-42

> *You have heard that it was said, "An eye for an eye and a tooth for a tooth." But I say to you, Do not resist the one who is evil. But if anyone slaps you on the right cheek, turn to him the other also. And if anyone would sue you and take your tunic, let him have your cloak as well. And if anyone forces you to go one mile, go with him two miles. Give to the one who begs from you, and do not refuse the one who would borrow from you.*

Turning the other cheek is very different from an eye for an eye. In all these statements in Matthew 5 He says *"but I say"* contrasting His statements with the ones Moses had given. He exerted the authority to rewrite what had come from Moses.

2) Mark 7:19

> *"...since it enters not his heart but his stomach, and is expelled?"* (Thus he declared all foods clean)

He declared all foods clean, thus overturning the many food prohibitions in the law.

3) Luke 9:54-55 (NKJV)

> *And when His disciples James and John saw this, they*

said, "Lord, do You want us to command fire to come down from heaven and consume them, just as Elijah did?" But He turned and rebuked them, and said, "You do not know what manner of spirit you are of."

Elijah had incinerated scores of soldiers that had come to arrest him. To do that now, in this era with Jesus, is to draw on a different spirit, not the Spirit of God.

4) Luke 4:18

*The Spirit of the Lord is upon me,
because he has anointed me
to proclaim good news to the poor.
He has sent me to proclaim liberty to the captives
and recovering of sight to the blind,
to set at liberty those who are oppressed...*

God in Christ came as healer, to give sight to the blind. In Exodus 4:11, God is giving some to see and some to be blind. We see this change played out in John 9:1-3:

As he passed by, he saw a man blind from birth. And his disciples asked him, "Rabbi, who sinned, this man or his parents, that he was born blind?" Jesus answered, "It was not that this man sinned, or his parents, but that the works of God might be displayed in him."

The assumption was that there was sin and blindness was the curse for it. Blind beggars were regularly spat on because of this belief. People were cursing those whom God had cursed. Jesus spat in the blind man's hearing, but not on him. He made mud from the spit and put it in the man's eyes and said that he should go wash. Jesus seems to be healing this man's experience of blindness in that culture as well as the blindness itself. Spit that once hurt and cursed now heals.

Jesus breaks with the thinking and practice based in the law that blindness was because of sin, either current or in the parental line. He gives sight to the blind.

5) Matthew 10:23

And you, Capernaum, will you be lifted up to the skies? No, you will go down to the depths. If the miracles that were performed in you had been performed in Sodom, it would have remained to this day.

Cities that were destroyed under the old system would be saved if they saw the miracles of God displayed in the new era. If they had seen the Son it would have changed the outcome! But they existed in a prior covenantal period.

6) John 8:4-5

they said to him, "Teacher, this woman has been caught in the act of adultery. Now in the Law Moses commanded us to stone such women. So what do you say?"

The law was clear: people caught in the act of adultery were stoned. Jesus sent her away with "Neither do I condemn you; go, and from now on sin no more." **Sin that meant death under the Law is now treated with leniency by Jesus. In Christ mercy triumphed over judgement.**

7) Matthew 8:2-3

And behold, a leper came to him and knelt before him, saying, "Lord, if you will, you can make me clean." And

> *Jesus stretched out his hand and touched him, saying, "I will; be clean." And immediately his leprosy was cleansed.*

The Law was clear. Lepers were to live outside the camp and not to be touched, otherwise you would become unclean. **Jesus touched them and made them clean.**

8) Mark 10:4-9

> *They said, "Moses allowed a man to write a certificate of divorce and to send her away." And Jesus said to them, "Because of your hardness of heart he wrote you this commandment. But from the beginning of creation, 'God made them male and female.' 'Therefore a man shall leave his father and mother and hold fast to his wife, and the two shall become one flesh.' So they are no longer two but one flesh. What therefore God has joined together, let not man separate."*

Jesus changed the perspective on divorce. He even says that the original text, inspired by God, had been given not because it represented God's heart or intention but because of the condition of the human heart. He gave them something they could cope with, but it did not represent His nature. Jesus rewrote the standard!

These eight examples illustrate with great clarity the massive change that Jesus introduced. Some of the shifts are difficult for those of us who like consistency because they stand in direct contrast with each other. But these shifts are nevertheless true. His thoughts and ways are truly above and beyond ours and we have to cope. They point to the huge shift in the way God was communicating to the planet. They are meant, I believe, to lead us to the conclusion the

New Testament writers came to. Jesus is the most accurate image of God ever; in fact He is *the* image of God.

4.4 The Only Sensible Conclusion

Everything that happened before Him was building toward His incarnation, setting the stage. The characters, prophecies and events that came before were types and shadows pointing ahead to Jesus as the reality (Colossians 2:17). As we see below, Paul, John and the writer to the Hebrews all agree on this vital point.

> He **is the image** of the invisible God, the firstborn over all creation. Colossians 1:15

> The Son is the radiance of God's glory and the exact representation of his being, sustaining all things by his powerful word. After he had provided purification for sins, he sat down at the right hand of the Majesty in heaven. John 14:9

> Anyone who has seen me has seen the Father. How can you say, "Show us the Father"?

> **In the beginning was the Word, and the Word was with God, and** the Word was God. John 1:1

We can legitimately assert that in these last days He has spoken to us through His Son and the Son is the full revelation of God. He is not a shadow to be replaced; He is the substance. He is what the Old Testament was both pointing to and getting us ready for.

Such is the force of these scriptures that you are led to the inevitable conclusion that if you can't find an aspect of God in Jesus, it's not in God. There's nothing left out and nothing in Him that should be removed. These verses support this idea: Jesus is perfect theology. When you study Him you study God in His fullness. His attitudes are God's attitudes and His activities perfectly express the Father's values. Jesus is God and is therefore the supreme revelation of His nature.

So Jesus is the lens we look at Bible history through, He shapes our paradigm, He gives us a way to interpret well what came before. We can see that some things in Bible history were for a season; they held sway in a certain covenantal era only to be replaced, adjusted or upgraded by the revelation that is the man Jesus Christ. Jesus trumps other views not because they aren't inspired but because He is the superior revelation. They were for a time, He is forever. Jesus Christ is the One who is yesterday, today and forever the same.

4.5 Is Heaven About to Fall?

One of our favourite story series as a family when the kids were growing was Asterix the Gaul. The Gauls had a magic potion which meant they could fight off any Roman invasion. They were indomitable, fearless, except for one thing. They were afraid that the sky might fall on their heads! Some of the things I have believed would make it likely that heaven could fall!

Jesus acted like David. David shifted the view of worship with his open display of the Ark of the Covenant as it was no longer hidden in the Holy of Holies. This was a radical, even potentially dangerous reinterpretation of God's ways. Jesus shifted the view of healing and the manifestation of the goodness of God. The book of Acts gives us a great summary verse for the ministry of Jesus, *"God anointed*

Is Heaven about to Collapse?

Jesus of Nazareth with the Holy Spirit and with power. He went about doing good and healing all who were oppressed by the devil, for God was with him" (Acts 10:38). This is the God we have come to know, the One who does good, who heals. The devil came to steal and kill and destroy; this God is the giver of abundant life. He is good and He does good.

We can confidently say Jesus is the perfect display of the will of God. Surely heaven is not a house divided against itself, and Jesus did not go about healing those the Father had made ill. He went around healing all who were oppressed of the devil. He was accused of healing and delivering people by the devil's power. His response was to say that was a dumb idea because that would mean Satan's house was divided against itself and it would therefore fall. Heaven is not about to fall through division between Father and Son.

The New Testament paradigm delivered by Jesus is that sickness isn't from God and healing is. This is a crunching gear change with some Old Testament ideas, which is why all the work we did on covenant and Jesus as the image of God is important. In this area He established a new standard, a fresh revelation. And we need to let it trump all others.

In the light of Jesus' wisdom, let's get our lines of thought in the right places. Jesus is healing, through the Father's love and power, people the devil has oppressed and made sick. The Father is not setting them up for Jesus to pull them down. The Father is not getting them sick for Jesus to heal them. That would be heaven's house divided against itself. It would mean that God the Trinity is working against Himself; He would be internally conflicted, which would lead to the collapse of the divine order!

You could hear from this that all sickness is from the devil, and yet although I believe he is the ultimate source of anything that steals or kills or destroys, sickness as we experience it can come from our fallen world, genetic problems, environmental problems etc. Jesus is able to heal all of them, whatever the presenting cause.

It really makes no sense to be told to go heal the sick, and for some of them to be ill because it's the Father's will. In James 5 when the sick are told to go to the elders for prayer it does not say "first discern if it's God's will" – it says that the prayer of faith will make the sick person well, no exception clauses. Jesus shows us the will of the Father.

4.6 New Covenant

There has been lots of debate about "healing in the atonement." What people mean is that, as Jesus atoned for our sin on the cross, did He at the same time atone for sickness? This is unhelpful because sin is a different issue and is wrapped up in human responsibility for sin and sinning, which needs forgiveness, needs cleansing, and needs "paying for" so that we might be declared righteous as a free gift. Healing is obviously related to disease, infirmity and disability. We may have responsibility for this, sin may be involved, but often that isn't the case. We are just ill and as we saw above, the source isn't the Lord.

Here we are talking about healing because of what was achieved on the cross and what was released by what Jesus did on the cross.

Here's Isaiah 53:3-6. The highlighted words are from the ESV margin (see also the NASB).

> *He was despised and rejected by men;*
>   *a man of **pains**, and acquainted with **sickness**;*
> *and as one from whom men hide their faces*
>   *he was despised, and we esteemed him not.*
> *Surely he has borne our **sickness***
>   *and carried our **pains**;*

Is Heaven about to Collapse?

> *yet we esteemed him stricken,*
>   *smitten by God, and afflicted.*
> *But he was wounded for our transgressions;*
>   *he was crushed for our iniquities;*
> *upon him was the chastisement that brought us peace,*
>   *and with his stripes we are healed.*
> *All we like sheep have gone astray;*
>   *we have turned – every one – to his own way;*
> *and the* L<small>ORD</small> *has laid on him*
>   *the iniquity of us all.*

Something very powerful happened at the cross in the realm of healing. As He bore our sin He also bore our sickness. By His wounds we are forgiven, by His stripes we are healed.

Part of our problem is seeing God as concerned with saving souls as the ultimate priority. If the really important and eternal bit of you is your soul, it's more important to God than your body. Your soul needs saving, and God cares about this so much that He sent his Son to die and bleed to cleanse you. But you are more than your soul. God doesn't have a greater passion for the unseen parts of you than the visible parts. He loves you, the complete you. If we do have parts, then He loves and deeply cares about all of them: spirit, soul and body. You are going to have a new body. Heaven isn't full of disembodied spirits. He likes bodies so much that Jesus still has one. I know it's a new and renewed one, but He is still incarnate in heaven. Having come in fallen human form, He now lives as first fruits in a redeemed human body! He loves your body and saves your body because He loves all of you, He made all of you (Revelation 1:13; Revelation 14:14; Hebrews 2:9).

Jesus wasn't just the sacrificial lamb. He was the covenant sacrifice; in His blood the bond of the New Covenant was made. It doesn't get more profound, serious or gruesome than God making Himself the bloody offering to ratify the covenant He is making. He bound Himself to us in His own blood. He bound God to man and man to God, and in that blood a promise was made and an inheritance secured; forgiven sin, cleansed sin and healed sickness. Jesus lived and died to demonstrate and establish the benefits of the Lord, to bind Himself to bless us with the benefits David had sung about centuries before:

Psalm 103:2-3

Bless the LORD, O my soul,
   and forget not all his benefits,
who forgives all your iniquity,
   who heals all your diseases…

Jesus is the answer to the question "Is it God's will to heal?" At the cross He made a sure and certain provision and promise for that healing.

4.7 Sickness and Suffering

Anyone who has suffered even a dose of the man flu knows sickness is suffering. Other diseases and infirmities bring us to places of great suffering which affect our bodies, our family and friends. Jesus was moved with compassion by such plights and healed the sufferers. As we have seen on our biblical journey, He came to do good, to heal, not destroy.

James 5 helps us in that it tells us if we are happy, to praise; if we are in trouble, to pray; and if we are sick, to call the elders and expect to get healed through the prayer of faith (James 5:13-16). Most people, even atheists, pray when they are in trouble. We hardly need the instruction! Here, though, James doesn't put sickness in the suffering category as many do, and I believe the lumping together of suffering and sickness is a mistake that continues to undermine faith to this day. The instruction is to get healing when you are sick, not endure the trial.

We are destined for trials and troubles, no question. Jesus actually made an unattractive promise that in the world you would have trouble. God is of course committed to the development of our character, and uses trials to grow faith and patience, etc.

The day we can expel the thought that God is making me ill to teach me something is the day many will rise up and walk in Jesus' name. God can use many circumstances to teach and train you. Sickness is not one of them – it's a different category, it puts you in line for a healing! The suffering created by sickness moves the Lord with compassion to heal. He suffered cruelly for us to have relief and healing.

Of course God can use anything, and prolonged sickness with no healing breakthrough can be used by God to do amazing things, but this doesn't legitimise the doctrine of "He's made me ill to teach me something," it simply shows His goodness and ability to turn the darkest things into light. In an era where we are still recovering healing, where there are many yet to be healed, we need to know His kindness, comfort and goodness in the waiting and the set-backs.

Not Everyone is Healed

This is the most perplexing part. But it's a problem of a generation, a wider culture. Don't blame yourself for lack of faith, and let no one else blame you either. If you are sick and still believing God, still clinging to hope for healing, you are a hero of faith!

Jesus' approach to those who struggled for breakthrough

was to rebuke the generation! He refers to a faithless generation when the disciples couldn't heal the boy. The Gospel writers also refer to the atmosphere of dishonour in Nazareth that inhibited Jesus' healing ministry. There's something in the atmosphere, something in the unbelieving nature of the whole group that can affect the flow of healing to individuals. If you are seeking healing, don't blame those around you; be a pioneer for a new generation, for an atmosphere of faith. Be a thermostat, setting the temperature, not a thermometer that just tells you what the temperature is right now. Don't quit on your hope – help us all move the agenda forward, help us all stop having the same debates and get on with healing the sick, raising the dead and cleansing the lepers. Be part of the breakthrough generation by staying in hope until your healing manifests.

God is about building a generation of believing believers, where healing will flow more easily than speaking in tongues or prophesying. Where faith is high in your church, your heart and in Christian culture in general. Let's celebrate the pioneers who face the pain, face the disappointments, but don't give up. They are laying a better foundation for themselves and those who are to follow.

Through this section we have gone on a biblical journey. We established the supremacy of Jesus as the full revelation of God by detailing the development of the covenants in the Old Testament, and showing how much shifted and changed in Christ. This helped us establish that the will of God is to heal the sick and not to make the healthy ill. We looked at how the New Testament categorises sickness separately from suffering. And we urged pioneers to keep hoping, keep praying and keep believing without being condemned for lack of faith, but commended for courage, as they press on for more breakthroughs.

Healing is already becoming more widespread in and through the Body of Christ, and with your engagement that is going to increase!

PART 5

WHY APOSTLES ARE FIRST

Apostles are making a comeback.

Their absence has left us with a lot of questions about their function, but they are vital to vibrant hope-filled Christianity, and to our experience of the fullness of Christ. We explore all that here.

5.1 Transforming Cities, Transforming Nations

Turkey and Mexico

A few years ago I stood in the spot Paul must have stood in 2,000 years earlier, outside the theatre in Ephesus in modern-day Turkey. Inside he could hear the crowd in the 25,000-seater amphitheatre; the shouting and near-riot lasted for over two hours, a demonstration stirred up by the city's silversmiths. Acts 19 gives us a graphic account of Paul and his companions turning a city upside down – a city of some 250,000 inhabitants with a world-renowned temple of the goddess Artemis.

Paul taught in Ephesus for two years and significant, extraordinary signs and wonders were done through him. Other city-impacting events recorded in Acts 19 included the failed deliverance attempt by the seven sons of Sceva and the subsequent brutal beating they took. This was then followed by the public burning of books of magic worth many thousands of pounds (the actual value is much debated; some estimate millions of pounds' worth).

What was really causing the stir for the silversmiths was that their jobs were at threat. People were turning away from the worship of Artemis and so their work creating shrines and idols was dwindling. The economy of the city was changing, the spiritual atmosphere of the city was changing and it created the setting for uproar. The men who were turning the world upside down were doing it here. Just as Jesus had taught, a sin city was repenting because of the signs it saw (Matthew 11:20-24).

I stood in that spot. I saw the Christian-coded inscriptions in many places along the street, I looked at the huge marketplace where the trinkets would have been sold, where the silversmiths made their money, and I was deeply affected. City transformation took place here and it will happen again.

Years earlier I had witnessed the transformation of a people group through signs and wonders. What had happened in biblical history happened to me and my friend Pete Carter.[a]

We went on a missions trip to the Pame Indians, up a remote mountain somewhere in the middle of Mexico. My goodness, these people were poor, scraping a living, no running water, living in stick huts on a hot bleak mountain. Most of the working-age men were over the border in the USA earning money, which they came home with and then drank away. These people were down at heel, with dreadful hopelessness in their eyes to the point that they wouldn't look at us. They walked by us staring at the ground.

Pete was a GP as well as a church leader and so we did doctor's rounds to huts and ran a clinic in the evening. The medical supplies he had were extremely limited. But some extraordinary stuff happened.

Otilio was an 18-year-old paralysed in all four limbs

because of brain damage. There was nothing in Pete's doctor's bag to help this guy, so he said "Let's pray." So we prayed. The young man was lying on a stick bed and he began to calm rather than twitch. Pete could tell this was an improvement and boldly helped the guy to his feet. It was so brilliant having medical eyes in this situation; I had no idea that what had started to happen was an improvement! He stood and walked for the first time in ten years. We were excited and stunned.

Clinic time arrived in early evening and there was a fair-sized queue. In the line was a mum carrying an 18-month-old. The baby looked to be in really bad shape. Pete could see she was dehydrated and was clearly suffering from dysentery brought on by the filthy water they drank. She was clinging to life. We prayed for a while and nothing seemed to change much. Pete gave her the antibiotics he had, knowing they wouldn't act in time.

Later that evening we had a meeting and the mum came with her baby. Pete couldn't find a pulse, and she was making a noise called the death rattle. She died. We prayed for about half an hour and something changed. Pete asked the mum to put the baby to her breast, and she fed! Life from death. The last I heard she was a healthy twelve-year-old girl!

These miracles, along with the excellent work of the young couple, Pepe and Vero, who were planting the church, changed the atmosphere. The next time we visited this people group, people smiled and gave us eye contact; their heads were up. The church grew to over three hundred in a people group of about fifteen thousand. Lots of positive changes happened to their living conditions, including the provision of water, housing and electricity. We had seen transformation in a people group, which was fantastic!

The early apostles' role in cultural formation was not

limited to the church. They were not creating little enclaves with strange practices to keep Christians safe. Their intention was to create the cities on a hill that Jesus talked about in Matthew 5. When He said they were "the light of the world" it wasn't in the sense of each individual being a light, but a city, a corporate light, a prominent influence; cities of God within the cities of men. Jesus envisaged that the corporate effect of His gathered disciples, His Church, would be a display of light. In the same way as He was the Light of the World, His gathered community was to display God's obvious glory to the earth. It would not be something hidden and hard to find, but obvious, attractive and illuminating.

Jesus chose the word *apostle* deliberately. He could have called his team priests or teachers or prophets. All these words were in play and understood at least by the Jewish community he was working within. But the noun "apostle" does not appear in the Septuagint (the Greek translation of the Old Testament) at all. *Apostle* is a Greek word and a Greek/Roman idea.

Kittel's *Theological Dictionary of New Testament Words* does an extensive job of defining the word from its Greek origin and cultural meaning, following it through to its Roman usage.[b]

The noun started life as a word describing cargo ships or a naval fleet being sent to new lands, then became used for those commanding those fleets, men sent from the homeland with the authority to represent it. It became linked to leaders in invading forces whose job was to enculturate the natives, not just defeat them. These were people authorised to spread Rome's culture, not just to militarily subdue new lands. The Roman mindset was to export Rome everywhere.

This potentially would have made the title difficult to bear for some Jewish young men as they were living in an occupied nation, a nation that was the subject of Romanisation by its "apostles." It does however explain more of what He meant when He taught them to pray that His will be done on earth as it is in heaven. They were to be heaven's ambassadors to see heaven's reality, heaven's ways, heaven's culture, established on the earth. As Rome sought to export its culture through its authorised representatives, they were culture establishers, culture exporters from heaven to earth, carrying the authorisation to do so.

Here are some of the final words of Jesus to His apostles:

*And Jesus came and said to them, "All authority in heaven and on earth has been given to me. Go therefore and **make disciples of all nations,** baptising them in the name of the Father and of the Son and of the Holy Spirit, teaching them to observe all that I have commanded you. And behold, I am with you always, to the end of the age."* Matthew 28:18-20

He didn't say to disciple individuals. Although that must be part of it, that wasn't the objective. He said to disciple nations. To be accurate He said to disciple people groups (*ethnos* is the Greek word here, and what we saw with the Pame was the transformation of a people group). Let's break this familiar passage down.

He told His disciples to baptise nations – we know this means to immerse or soak – in the name of the Father, Son and Spirit. The secondary meaning can be baptising individuals, but we have made it primary. The context is clearly nations. Is Jesus envisaging some grand baptismal service of millions? Perhaps, but the idea is to baptise them in the "name."

The "name" speaks of the authority of the Trinity. Somehow nations were to be discipled by an immersion in the authority of the Godhead. Jesus had displayed what this was like because He came in the name of the Father. He came with heaven's authority. If you were around Him for any length of time you were immersed in a display of Heaven's authority. Whole towns were immersed in an experience of the display of Trinitarian love and power that happened through Jesus.

We talk these days about "immersive" experiences – multimedia presentations or virtual reality headsets that engage multiple senses at the same time. These media technologies "baptise" you into the computer game or video you are watching. If you were with Jesus as you handed out the bread to the five thousand and it multiplied in your hands, you were immersed!

Such was the grandeur of Jesus' view of the authority He had delegated to His followers; He had no doubt that nations could be transformed as they exercised that authority in the way He did.

They were to soak these nations with the governmental realities of heaven, saturate them with the reality of His kingdom. Not as domination, but as a display, as salt and as light, as leaven, permeating every aspect of life: society, government and culture. What a vision He has for His Church!

Paul put it like this in his letter to the Ephesians. He said God raised Jesus up:

...far above all rule and authority and power and dominion, and above every name that is named, not only in this age but also in the one to come. And he put all things under his feet and gave him as head over all things to the church, which is his body, the fullness of him who fills all in all. Ephesians 1:21-23

His authority was established for the Church, so the Church could bring about transformation on the earth. It makes sense that His apostles were commissioned as nation-changers; people who were authorised to turn the world upside down.

What Paul experienced in Ephesus, and what we experienced in a seed form in Mexico, represent what Jesus has commissioned the apostolic to do.

5.2 Foundations

> *According to the grace of God given to me, like a skilled master builder I laid a foundation, and someone else is building upon it. Let each one take care how he builds upon it. For no one can lay a foundation other than that which is laid, which is Jesus Christ.* 1 Corinthians 3:10-11

Paul the apostle laid a foundation for others to build on. He laid it in a specific church in the city of Corinth. It required a special grace to do this, the skill of a master builder. The question is: what is that foundation? The foundation is of course Jesus, but what is a "foundation of Jesus" in a church? Can we take this beyond the classic Sunday School answer?

I would like to suggest this is the tangible presence of Jesus.

Paul says it's a foundation already laid, and yet it has to be laid in every church. What does this mean? It means the work of Jesus is done; He suffered the brutish cross, has risen and ascended, and His presence has been given to us. He said He will never leave us or forsake us (Matthew 28:19-20), He said He would give His Spirit once He was glorified (John 7:39). Now that He is glorified, the reality of the Spirit's presence needs to be realised and enjoyed in every congregation as the founding reality of that community.

This "foundation already laid" can't mean a correct idea or

a correct doctrine of Christ as that was not already laid. Paul had come to lay the foundation that he had the revelation of. He came to give them the truth of Christ that they might experience the presence of Christ. It has to be nothing less than Christ himself, His living presence manifest among them. The Church is not just built for His presence, but on His presence!

Of course unhelpful teaching that brings guilt and shame, that builds walls of separation between heaven and earth, between us and God, can work against realising this reality. We need teaching and preaching that create the faith and space for the Holy Spirit to manifest and show us Jesus.

Wholesome teaching brings to people's understanding that there is now freedom from separation and condemnation; that God is near, reconciliation has happened, distance has been cancelled. The fruit of that kind of declaration is ease in His presence; faith for Him to be there in tangible ways. As an apostle Paul keeps teaching and presence, Word and Spirit, connected. He contends for an experiential Christ as the foundation of the local community of believers. This experience is rooted in both the proclamation of Jesus' death, resurrection and outpoured Spirit, and the actual demonstration of the activity of the Spirit among them.

What he has already said to them in 1 Corinthians 2 backs this up and harmonises the speaking and teaching element of Paul's ministry with the experiential reality it brought.

And I, when I came to you, brothers, did not come proclaiming to you the testimony of God with lofty speech or wisdom. For I decided to know nothing among you except Jesus Christ and him crucified. And I was with you in weakness and in fear and much trembling, and my speech and my message were not in plausible words of wisdom, but in demonstration of the Spirit and of power, that your faith might not rest in the wisdom of men but in the power of God. 1 Corinthians 2:1-5

Their faith was not built on a foundation of human wisdom, on words alone, but on words that carried with them a demonstration of the Spirit's power. Words can be powerful in and of themselves, especially the preaching of Christ and His cross. But Paul considered the full proclamation to include signs and wonders (Romans 15:19 NIV and NASB). Their faith was built on the experience of the reality of the words.

In Paul's experience there was no separation of Word and Spirit, of proclamation and demonstration, or of explanation and experience. The separation of ideas from experiences does not reflect New Testament reality and we would do well to seek the restoration of the New Testament norm. We are not building our lives or our churches on great biblical ideas, apart from biblical encounter and biblically proportioned experiences of the Spirit. If we do, our faith will be weakened and we will tend toward an intellectual belief that doesn't carry the level of conviction that is produced by experiential faith.

I was alerted to this reality when I was speaking at a healing conference a few years back. At the end of the meeting people came forward for healing and one or two were healed, but nothing particularly noteworthy at the time. I stayed on and after the next session a lady found me and said that during the talk I had given she started to realise her back and hips had realigned, her legs had become the same length and her pain had gone. She had spent the last session walking and testing her healing. She'd been healed without prayer, listening to the preaching. I was amazed. A couple of weeks later I spoke at a different church. I didn't speak on healing. At the end the leader came up to me and introduced me to a man who was maybe in his late 50s or into his 60s. The man said he had come in with a hip problem which meant he slightly dragged one leg, and during the talk he'd been healed, which he then demonstrated. This happening once was exciting; twice got my attention. I've learned that these repeat experiences are often God trying to get my attention.

En-route to the next place we were going to minister, we were challenging each other to take risks. This time I finished my message and said "Hands up if you came with pain today." Five people put their hands up and said what had been wrong. I then said "Check it out, for someone is already healed." Pains in hands disappeared, one guy who had come to the meeting with stomach problems instantly recovered; others said they were feeling better. I think this was Word and Spirit!

5.3 All About His Presence

Apostles are fundamentally presence bringers, presence carriers and presence establishers. The first people called apostles in the New Testament were the twelve disciples. The primary directive to them was as follows:

> And he called to him his twelve disciples and gave them authority over unclean spirits, to cast them out, and to heal every disease and every affliction. The names of the twelve apostles are these: first, Simon, who is called Peter, and Andrew his brother; James the son of Zebedee, and John his brother; Philip and Bartholomew; Thomas and Matthew the tax collector; James the son of Alphaeus, and Thaddaeus; Simon the Cananaean, and Judas Iscariot, who betrayed him. These twelve Jesus sent out, instructing them, "Go nowhere among

Why Apostles are First

the Gentiles and enter no town of the Samaritans, but go rather to the lost sheep of the house of Israel. And proclaim as you go, saying, 'The kingdom of heaven is at hand.' **Heal the sick, raise the dead, cleanse lepers, cast out demons.** *You received without paying; give without pay. Acquire no gold nor silver nor copper for your belts, no bag for your journey, nor two tunics nor sandals nor a staff, for the labourer deserves his food. And whatever town or village you enter, find out who is worthy in it and stay there until you depart. As you enter the house, greet it. And if the house is worthy,* **let your peace come upon it, but if it is not worthy, let your peace return to you.** *And if anyone will not receive you or listen to your words, shake off the dust from your feet when you leave that house or town. Truly, I say to you, it will be more bearable on the day of judgement for the land of Sodom and Gomorrah than for that town."*
Matthew 10:1-15

The original apostolic mandate is in the realm of announcing and displaying the kingdom of God. I still find verse 8 a challenge to us as church. Even though we see some breakthrough, there's much more for us to reach the basic standard of the first mission trip of the Bible. Raising the dead, anyone?

Where the King is, there is the kingdom. The presence of the King's authority delegated to the apostles was displayed. Where His presence is looks like healing, deliverance, signs and wonders and changed lives. It's beyond a warm feeling.

They were also instructed to "let their peace come upon it." This is a slightly strange concept to Westerners. It speaks of an atmosphere, something the apostles had or carried that they could deposit in a house or take back.

Peace is a reference to the idea of Shalom that we see in

the Old Testament. In Isaiah 9:6-7 Jesus is called the Prince of Peace (shalom) and we are told that of the increase of His government and peace (shalom) there will be no end. Shalom is a bigger idea than just a lack of agitation or the presence of peacefulness. It means wellbeing in its broadest sense; it means prosperity and health. The increase of Jesus' government was to be side by side with an increase in shalom! The apostles released wellbeing into places that were receptive. You could say they changed the atmosphere in the houses they visited. You can deposit wellbeing in a person or household that is receptive.

We did a mission trip to the east of France. On our first night a lady came forward for prayer for a ten-year-old back injury. The doctors said that only surgery could fix it, but she didn't fancy the risk. She was on ten doses of strong painkillers per day. We prayed and all the pain left. The next day she came in having not slept all night because she had been praising God for her newfound freedom. We asked her to pray for a guy in that meeting with an unspecified heart problem.

A year later Jan, one of our team and a powerful supernatural catalyst, returned to the area and met the woman. The woman told her that after we left other conditions in her body we knew nothing about started to heal. First her knees recovered, then her diabetes got healed and then her eyesight started to improve. She also said that the guy with the heart problem had been healed as well! That's increasing shalom/wellbeing.

And God has appointed in the church first apostles, second prophets, third teachers, then miracles, then gifts of healing, helping, administrating, and various kinds of tongues. 1 Corinthians 12:28

The instruction to have apostles first is to ensure that what we have described above is the reality. Plenty of other things can come in and become a foundation if this isn't laid first. The founding, directing reality of the church is the presence of God. This is first apostles because the foundations they lay belong in the ground first, before the building goes on top. This is not first in a prominence sense or first as the head of a hierarchy. The foundation isn't growth or even discipleship, as important as these are. The fundamental dynamic of the church community is Christ Himself, not stuff we do.

This foundation resonates and reflects Jesus' own ministry and the way He commissioned the first apostles.

Of course doctrine is important, but apostles are not teaching truths for people to remember and refer to as key truths, but teaching them so people encounter the living reality of the person expressed in and through the truths. From this flows transformed lives.

The apostles are not primary in the sense of them being "over everything and everyone," but first because the grace they have is needed first. It's a grace to establish the experiential reality of Jesus in a community as its living foundation.

5.4 Apostolic Teaching

Context is vital in interpreting scripture. Diligent Bible readers will look at the verses before and after a text they are thinking about, and good Bible study will lead you to explore and understand the cultural and historic context of the authors and readers. All of this helps us get an accurate understanding of a text. We also further our understanding by working hard at the meaning of the Greek and Hebrew words, to get an accurate sense of their meaning in the context used.

I am so thankful for the incredible work of scholars, Bible translators and theologians who seek to help us comprehend the sense and depth of scripture; they give us great commentaries and Bible study tools. I am amazed though that another type of context is often ignored. That is the spiritual experience of the authors. I am particularly thinking New Testament epistles here, but it does apply across the board.

When I was a young Christian we did a Bible study on the spiritual gifts listed in 1 Corinthians 12. The study was authored by people who didn't believe gifts still existed in the supernatural way the text described. They managed to get these passages to refer to the natural skills and abilities that God had given us. This obviously poor bit of explanation sparked my interest in what these gifts might really be. It was clear that the authors had no grid for what they had read in the biblical text; as a result they had massaged the text into a meaning they did have a reference point for. They naturalised it, and squeezed it into the paradigm they were familiar with. I wanted to know why, and what the real deal was, which actually contributed to me getting baptised in the Spirit and speaking in tongues!

It's difficult, in fact impossible, for someone who has never spoken in tongues to do an accurate job of exegeting 1 Corinthians 12-14.

How can we accurately interpret Paul or Peter or John if we have none of their experiences in our lives? Doesn't an apostolic teacher need apostolic experiences?

Here's Paul in Ephesians 3:1-8 talking about the truth he preached and how he received it; note the highlighted words.

> *For this reason I, Paul, a prisoner for Christ Jesus on behalf of you Gentiles—assuming that you have heard of the stewardship of God's grace that was given to me*

> *for you, how **the mystery was made known to me by revelation**, as I have written briefly. When you read this, you can perceive my insight into the mystery of Christ, which was not made known to the sons of men in other generations as it has **now been revealed to his holy apostles and prophets by the Spirit**. This mystery is that the Gentiles are fellow heirs, members of the same body, and partakers of the promise in Christ Jesus through the gospel.*
>
> *Of this gospel I was made a minister according to the gift of God's grace, which was **given me by the working of his power**. To me, though I am the very least of all the saints, this grace was given, to preach to the Gentiles the unsearchable riches of Christ...*

In Acts 22:17, 2 Corinthians 12:1 and Galatians 1:12, Paul tells us he had many visions and revelations of the Lord and that these were so extreme in nature that he received a 'thorn' to help him not be too carried away! No human taught him; his gospel was not the product of his religious education, but revelation.

Here are some of the apostle John's experiences:

> *I was **in the Spirit** on the Lord's day, **and I heard** behind me a loud voice like a trumpet saying, "Write what you see in a book and send it to the seven churches, to Ephesus and to Smyrna and to Pergamum and to Thyatira and to Sardis and to Philadelphia and to Laodicea."* Revelation 1:10-11

And Peter:

> *I was in the city of Joppa praying, and **in a trance I saw a vision**, something like a great sheet descending, being*

let down from heaven by its four corners, and it came down to me. Looking at it closely, I observed animals and beasts of prey and reptiles and birds of the air. And I heard a voice saying to me, "Rise, Peter; kill and eat." But I said, "By no means, Lord; for nothing common or unclean has ever entered my mouth." But the voice answered a second time from heaven, "What God has made clean, do not call common." This happened three times, and all was drawn up again into heaven. Acts 11:5-10

The men who wrote very significant parts of our New Testament had no New Testament. They did have what Jesus had promised though: the Holy Spirit, the teacher and leader into all truth. They were men familiar with hearing from God through heavenly encounters and trusting the information they received.

Do present-day apostles have access to the same grace on their lives as the early apostles? Of course the original Twelve are unique, as the apostles of the Lamb. But does the modern-day apostolic gift have access to less grace than a first-century one? I believe they need the same grace to see and steward the mysteries of Christ, a grace to experience the encounters the original authors had and so be able to bring that revelation to their generation. There is no question here of adding to scripture, just accurately interpreting it experientially and contextually, being able to have greater understanding of what we read and study on the pages of the Bible because we share in the same kind of experiences as the authors.

The background of much of western Christianity in cessationism has perhaps blinded us to the need and availability of apostolic revelatory experiences in the present day. In cessationism, which believes such people have ceased to exist as gifts to the Body of Christ, the belief system insists their level of encounter must have passed away too. I would suggest that both apostles and apostolic encounters like trances, dreams and visions are being restored. These experiences better equip present-day apostles to interpret the sense of the original authors in whose footsteps they tread. Present-day apostles aren't writing new New Testaments but encountering the author in authentic experiences which more profoundly reveal the truth of the recorded words. With unveiled faces they behold the glory of the Lord in all His truth.

This does not remove the need for study, theology and great thinking, but study and thinking on its own will not bring us to the full revelation of Christ as was intended by the Lord when He began giving His gifts to men. When the more cerebral activities are separated from the experiential, they lead us toward leaning on wise and persuasive words, or gaining knowledge that simply fills our minds. Paul wisely said that knowledge alone can puff us up and lead us to a sense of superiority.

Apostolic teaching defines Christian culture

Some years ago I heard British apostle Terry Virgo speak about Acts 2:42. What he said about the role of the apostles and their teaching inspired and informed the following:

The early church was birthed inside of Judaism, inside the customs and beliefs of Old Covenant people. In its early development it was seen as a sect of Judaism. It was also birthed in a Roman-dominated world. Roman culture and thinking had many of its roots in Greek thinking.

What was the Church? Where did it fit in the culture and beliefs of its day?

What the apostles taught did such a good job of defining the new and distinct space in which the Church existed that they managed to upset both the major cultures they were living in, and so they ended up being violently persecuted by Jews and Romans alike. The culture of heaven that the apostles taught challenged and conflicted with the other cultures the Church was birthed into. Quickly the Church, Christianity, became a thing in its own right and was rejected by what was around it. In Antioch they were first called Christians. In that sense, they were given a distinct new name.

The challenge of defining the Church in the context it is living in remains for every generation and so today apostles are required for the same reasons as in the first century. They are needed to define the culture of Christianity so that it doesn't become consumed by popular culture, or stuck in any unhelpful elements inherited from its religious past. To avoid religious inertia and irrelevance or cultural syncretism, we need apostles today. It is vital that we have apostles who know the scriptures and regularly encounter the risen Lord in visions and other revelatory experiences.

5.5 The Apostolic Ministry of Jesus

> *Therefore, holy brothers, you who share in a heavenly calling, consider Jesus, the apostle and high priest of our confession...* Hebrews 3:1

Have you considered Jesus as an apostle, the first of His kind? He set a pretty challenging standard.

As I studied what He did and what was the fruit of His earthly ministry, I noticed a role He performed which I hadn't heard talked about before. He prepared His followers for Pentecost. He prepared them to recognise, receive and run with the Holy Spirit as He was poured out.

I searched the Old Testament and couldn't find a text that described what happened in Acts 2. There is the promise of

Why Apostles are First

the outpouring of the Spirit, but no check list, nothing you could refer to that would let you know "this is it" from an external viewpoint. Yet Peter confidently said "this is what was uttered through the prophet Joel." How did he know? The phenomena that accompanied the outpouring were strange.

There was the sound of a rushing wind that was so loud it gathered a crowd, but no actual wind. There was fire on people's heads and strange languages in their mouths. According to many onlookers their behaviour was drunken at 9am.

The onlookers on the day of Pentecost responded with a mixture of amazement, perplexity and mockery. The crowd had no unanimous view on what was taking place. The disciples received what God was doing and didn't resist or run with fear. The Twelve stood together with Peter. They knew it was God because Jesus had trained them to not be put off by their natural senses but perceive the work of the Spirit accurately.

In this day and age I suspect such phenomena would scare many believers. There would be amazement, perplexity and perhaps mockery. Within some churches a new Pentecost could be hard to handle. If anything close to the original happened some churches would split. Imagine you are singing in worship one Sunday morning and there is a noise like a jet engine or a hurricane, fire appears on your neighbour's head, and lots of people start staggering around babbling in strange languages. I think there would be great debates about whether it was all from God or not. The leadership would inspect the air-conditioning checking for faults. Someone would call the local air traffic control to see if there had been any low-flying aircraft. Maybe they would breathalyse the congregation and check everyone's language qualifications. However, you look at this, it's a major departure from what normally qualifies for "decently and in order"!

Jesus' disciples were rock solid, embracing what was happening without a flicker of fear. They had been equipped by Jesus to recognise the presence and work of the Spirit, receive it and run with it. Think of all the strange things He put them through: scary trips across stormy lakes to encounter crazed and dangerous possessed people who broke chains with their bare hands, people tearing off roofs to lower cripples into the middle of meetings, voices from God some people thought were thunder, and to top it all there were the crowd-pleasing sermons telling people they had to eat His flesh and drink His blood.

Jesus' training course in the bizarre and scary had prepared them. Being around the man who had the Spirit without measure, and being used by God powerfully themselves, meant they were ready. Jesus said in John 14 that they already knew the Holy Spirit: *"You know him, for he dwells with you and will be in you."* He dwelled with them because He, the Spirit of the Sovereign Lord, was on Jesus in limitless measure, and they saw His actions and felt His presence (Luke 4:18).

The preparation of the disciples to accurately recognise the work of the Spirit, however it looked, was an expression of His apostolic ministry. An overlooked legacy of Jesus was His disciples' ability to discern the Spirit. I would suggest that this forms part of the function of modern-day apostles. Their anointing and the works they do prepare people to recognise and receive the work of the Holy Spirit. It's a key part of training people that is often overlooked. The outcome of not training is that people often respond to Holy Spirit activity by assessing its external affects, what they can see and hear, rather than discerning the spirit behind the activity. It is so important to train our senses and activate spiritual discernment in its positive sense, and not just be those who use our natural senses and minds. Using the natural senses usually triggers fear, even when it's actually God. Discerning His authentic presence ignites faith. Solid food is for the mature, for those who have their powers of discernment **trained** by constant practice to distinguish good from evil (Hebrews 5:14).

Church history is full of people who rejected revival because of the strange phenomena that accompanied it. They didn't like how it looked – how it looked couldn't be God. Apostolic ministry has a key role in preparing people to connect to God however He manifests. The goal is to equip God's people to activate their spiritual discernment so they embrace outpourings and not reject them because of the phenomena that accompany them.

Apostles are key to creating wineskins and environments that can recognise, receive and run with outpourings from heaven.

5.6 Apostles, Not Teachers, First

Commenting on 1 Corinthians 12:28, Bible scholar Gordon Fee makes the following remark: "But the question of authority structures is not asked here and in terms of the argument is altogether irrelevant. It is of some note that those most interested in this question have relegated the first two ministries to the first century only, so that the third, teacher, now assumes the first position. One wonders whether a teacher first designed this hermeneutics" (*God's Empowering Presence*, p190, note 397).

Jesus left eleven apostles to found the first churches and advance His kingdom on the earth. From their influence we start to see the emergence of other gifts in the book of Acts. We see prophets mentioned three times, teachers once (in Antioch, Acts 13:1) and evangelists once (Philip in Acts 8). Jesus didn't start with teachers but apostles. From the environment they created came teachers, prophets and evangelists.

Paul laid hands on elders and exhorted them to shepherd the flock of God, but sadly there are no examples of pastors as a distinct individual with that gift in the New Testament. As a gift it gets a single mention in Ephesians 4:11.

These statistics made me re-evaluate my priorities. We are on the verge of being obsessive about pastors and teachers in our modern church culture. We have worship pastors, children's pastors, senior pastors, assistant pastors etc. The New Testament emphasis is on establishing apostolic ministry as the priority, followed by prophets.

My contention would be that if teachers or pastors are first, in the sense that they are the primary gift that sets the atmosphere and they define the parameters and boundaries of a church or ministry, it is then suffocating for prophets, apostles and often evangelists. Apostles, however, create a world in which all gifts can flourish if they will buy into the fundamental foundation of the apostle as described above. There is much teaching in the New Testament, but it is apostles doing it; we cannot use the abundant nature of teaching in our New Testament to justify the need for teachers above everything else. That's applying an assumption to the texts driven by the kind of paradigm Gordon Fee alludes to above.

Few prophets succeed in local churches and it's usually because they are in environments created by teachers and pastors. Apostles are the only people who can really live with prophets! There's a unique grace to bind apostles and prophets together. Breaking that link can do serious harm to the dynamic of the church (Ephesians 2:20; Ephesians 3:5) and the success of the apostles and prophets. There are of course prophets and teachers in the leadership team of five in Antioch, and in those five there were two emerging apostles in Barnabas and Paul. No one person in that team is identified as the team leader and there is no assumption of the primacy of the teachers in the team.

5.7 Apostolic Authority

Paul, an apostle—not from men nor through man, but through Jesus Christ and God the Father, who raised him from the dead... Galatians 1:1

Saul of Tarsus was Paul from heaven. Saul became Paul, a man authorised directly by Jesus and God the Father. He was not sent or authorised by any human agency. If you need human agency to authorise you as an apostle, you either don't believe your call and encounter, or you aren't an apostle. Direct, profound authorisation and sending by God are the source of true apostolic authority. If apostles are establishing heaven's culture on earth as its representatives, they need that kind of authority. Leaning on derived authority will not hack it.

This can make us feel like these are superheroes, untouchable in their authorisation, strong and independent. What's helpful is Paul wasn't independent. He'd been sent by a church, his calling recognised by the senior leadership at Antioch. He didn't see that affirmation as his source of authority, though. He had a direct call from God and combined that with a real connection to leadership in a local church. The two things sit in harmony together and make a powerful combination.

<u>What kind of authority</u>

In Matthew 8 we read the story of the centurion whose servant was healed. Now this man stunned Jesus by his faith because he had some incredible insight into Jesus' authority. He could see that a word from Jesus would mean sickness and disease had to leave; it was under His authority in the same way the soldiers were under his authority as a centurion, when he said "go" they had to go. His experience of a human hierarchy gave him a window into Jesus' authority over demons and sickness. There was no argument, obedience was not optional. The demons in the Gadarene demoniac were under no doubt they had to go; they just wanted to negotiate favourable exit terms! This is authority "over." And it's probably linked to the voluntary submission of the Lord to His Father for the earthly mission of salvation. Because of the spirit realm dominion Jesus obviously carried, distance was clearly no object in the centurion's mind. He had faith in Jesus' spiritual authority.

Early in Acts the apostles start to move in this kind of influence too.

In Acts 3 Peter and John at the Gate Beautiful said, "Silver and gold we do not have but what **I have** I give to you, in the Name (authority) of Jesus rise and walk." In the same way that they were certain they had no cash on them that day, they knew they had something more tangible and more relevant, authority to heal.

The centurion's words can't be interpreted as justification for "top down" authority over people in church structures because Jesus expressly forbade that kind of exercise of authority.

> But Jesus called them to him and said, "You know that the rulers of the Gentiles **lord it over them**, and their great ones **exercise authority over them. It shall not be so among you**. But whoever would be great among you must be your servant, and whoever would be first

among you must be your slave, even as the Son of Man came not to be served but to serve, and to give his life as a ransom for many." Matthew 20:25-18

Jesus was not affirming a Roman military-style authoritarianism for His church in His response to the centurion, but the faith of a man who saw His authority over sickness.

Apostolic authority as Paul saw it was "for" people, not "over" them. Authority for building them up. You need authority to represent heaven and manifest it on earth, but it's never enforced. People get to choose. Demons and sickness don't have an option, we do "lord it" over them, but never one another.

For even if I boast a little too much of our authority, which the Lord gave for building you up and not for destroying you, I will not be ashamed. 2 Corinthians 10:8

It takes authority to teach and establish leadership, even to establish churches. This is authority for people, to strengthen, establish and even protect.

The only place in the New Testament I can find where one human is encouraged to have authority over another is in the marriage bed, and even there it's mutual! (1 Corinthians 7:4.)

Submission

Submission, however, is commanded in scripture in the realm of human relationships. Wives are exhorted to submit to their husbands, but it doesn't say for husbands to rule their wives, it says to love them. Submission to secular leaders is also commanded, and the secular leaders don't have to be nice to qualify for our honour (see Roman 13:1-7; Hebrews 13:17; 1 Thessalonians 5:17). Submission, or openness to reason, is seen as healthy and a component of heavenly wisdom (James 3:17).

I find this profound. None are permitted to rule over, even though leadership authority exists, but all are called to submit. Beautiful. This requires a voluntary appreciation of all the gifts and graces in the people around you, especially the leadership ones. If leaders have authority **for you,** then to not appreciate the grace they have is to miss out on what they can supply **to you**. They must not insist or force; the posture of our heart toward them is ours to maintain. The goal is not a response to a position or title, although positions and even titles exist for the sake of organisational clarity, but a valuing of gift and grace.

Apostolic leaders governing over, ruling over, lording over in the expectation of compliance because they are in a position of authority is forbidden by Jesus. Voluntary submission and honour of those with leadership gifting is encouraged as the way to benefit from the grace given to those leaders to enrich your life in God.

Endnotes
a. For a fuller account of these events read Pete's excellent book *Unwrapping Lazarus*.
b. If you want to research this, make sure you don't use the abridged version of Kittel's.

PART 6

HOPES AND DREAMS

Hope deferred makes the heart sick, but a desire fulfilled is a tree of life. Proverbs 13:12

A sick heart does not have to be the outcome of a disappointing week or a disappointing life.

Our Heavenly Father is freeing hearts that they might dream with Him again.

Heaven is coming to earth through your vibrant hopes and dreams.

6.1 Disappointment Does Not Have to Mean Lost Hope

Hope tends to be seen as a wish; something bright and optimistic, but not necessarily possible or at all certain. In biblical terms though, hope is not a wish but the certain expectation of good from a good God.

The Proverb shows us that hope is a crucial ingredient to a healthy heart because deferred hope leads to heart sickness. Heart sickness can look like many things. It can look like an inner collapse under the weight of disappointment. It can look like doubting the faithfulness of God, even accusing

God. It can become bitterness toward God, or even toward people who got in the way of the dream.

A sick heart is not a great place. It struggles to love and incubate hope and faith. It really is the spring of our lives.[a]

Letting go of hope, that is, deferring hoping to another day in the future, is what actually sickens the heart. Of course this can be triggered by a failed expectation, a disappointment. But there is a difference between letting go of hope and being disappointed. One does not follow automatically from the other. The scripture doesn't say disappointment makes the heart sick. Disappointment is something we naturally feel, but we get to choose whether or not we defer or ditch our hope for a more opportune time.

Biblical hope is meant to work against hope. Abraham, against hope, hoped! (Romans 4:18) This means he was surrounded by circumstances that should discourage hope, but hoped anyway. The hope we are talking about is not attached to the opportune nature of the time you are in, it's designed to create a future opportune moment. This is because it's attached to the one who breathed the hope into us. It has the power to actually fashion a spot in the future when hope can be realised and desire fulfilled.

Hebrews 11:1 puts it this way: *"Faith is the assurance of things hoped for."* In that sense hope precedes faith, creates an internal environment for faith to happen.

I can steward my heart. I can watch over it, I have power to protect and guard what enters my heart. Like a gardener, I cannot allow unhealthy weeds to take root in the garden of my heart. Because it is the spring of my life (Proverbs 4:23) it is vital I don't have a fatalistic attitude to the condition of my heart. What will be does not have to be as far as my inner life is concerned. I have the ability to let into it what is healthy and keep unhealthy stuff out. I get to choose to keep hope alive, and so sustain a healthy heart.

Because I thought it was disappointment that made the heart sick, I developed life and church strategies to limit the possibility of disappointment. But this meant aiming low, keeping expectations small and realistic in order to protect myself and others from the pain of disappointment. And this strategy can look like wisdom from on high, but what I discovered is that it insulated me from receiving more of heaven.

I also thought sickness of heart was just the natural and normal outcome of disappointment; I didn't know I had a choice. The trouble with that view is that it puts you and me into a place where we feel destined to accumulate ever increasing mounds of disappointment in our hearts, as if to live life with its ups and downs equals a guaranteed sick heart. Jesus said the opposite. He said you would have trouble in the world – one of His less popular promises – but to be of good cheer. And the reason for cheer is His overcoming of the world.

You should abandon hope, you have every reason on earth to give up, or so say your circumstances. Circumstances can speak loudly to you, trusted friends can reason with you, every voice from your history can call to you, "you're foolish to continue to hope." But every reason on earth cannot outweigh every reason in heaven. Against hope Abraham hoped.

God is full of Hope (Romans 15:13), and if you think for a moment you'll realise the devil is the opposite, he's hopeless. The devil is in a hopeless state. Both he and God are recruiting! Don't let the heavy weight of earthly disappointments recruit you to the hopeless party. Just as our Heavenly Father is the God of all hope, the devil is the source of hopelessness. If you are feeling hopeless, it's not from heaven.

If we lose hope we eventually lose vibrant faith and

expectation. We then can't move forward and ultimately we stop pleasing God, because without faith it's impossible to please Him (Hebrews 11:3).

Hope has its roots and sustenance in God, His nature and His promises. Its anchor is heaven. His love hopes all things. When we go to Him with our disappointments, He is the comforter. There is understanding, strength and also renewal of hope for us in His heart.

Abraham's solution is the best one:

No distrust made him waver concerning the promise of God, but he grew strong in his faith as he gave glory to God, fully convinced that God was able to do what he had promised. That is why his faith was "counted to him as righteousness." Romans 4:20-22

Where his circumstances were pushing strongly in the opposite direction to the promises, he gave glory to God. He worshipped, he chose hope over hopelessness. It is what righteousness looks like. It can feel painful and unnatural to worship and give thanks when it looks like it's all going down the toilet. But we are learning to turn our affections to Him, learning to let His mood be ours and His promises remain certain to us in times of setback. In this place of sacrificial praise, hope and faith actually grow despite the contrary circumstances. You don't need answers and breakthroughs to grow in faith!

Disappointment has its origins in this fallen earth, in the difficulties of a broken planet and an active devil. To allow it to rule my heart condition is to allow my heart to be "earthed." My perspective shifts from heaven's possibilities and resources to the earth's limitations.

Hopelessness can be in a person, a national culture or a family line. It can come from economic problems, persistent sickness, wars and relational tensions and breakdown. It can be in churches, leaking in from the surrounding culture or just simply because of church problems; lack of breakthrough, relational tensions, sickness...wars? Yes, all the same things that affect a nation or family can infect a church culture.

But nothing is actually without hope. If you are sick, there is hope of healing; if you are dying there is hope of heaven and His face; if you are dead there is hope of resurrection; if you are broke there is hope of provision; if you are depressed there is hope of joy; if everything seems lost there is the hope of His love that never fails and from which we cannot be separated. There's always a promise, always a word from the Father, always something that points to a better outcome. And not just in heaven, but also on earth. The better outcome can seem so unlikely as to be laughable at the time, unbelievable, but it will come to pass as we cling to hope.

6.2 Hope for Good Things

God is good. No one would argue with that as a theological statement. But I found I had disconnected His good nature from goodness itself. The Bible clearly states not only that God is good but also that every good and perfect gift comes from Him. All good things come from a good God! There is no other source of goodness in the universe – not the enemy, not your uncle, not chance or luck.

Your uncle, or your boss, or however the good thing came to you, are channels for His goodness, not the ultimate source. Think! Every good thing, wherever it is found, comes from Him. There is no other origin.

EVERY good thing comes from Him. Goodness is expressed in good things. The psalmist puts it this way:

"Taste and see that God is good." His good nature can be experienced in good things.

It felt like somewhere in our evangelical roots we had assigned all goodness from God to spiritual things like salvation and forgiveness and left out His goodness expressed in the material world and so limited our expectation of goodness from a good God – we shrank our hope. Yet it's Him who makes the sun to shine on the righteous and unrighteous alike.

We realised our belief system had some Gnostic tendencies. Gnosticism was a heresy the early church struggled with, and its influence is still being felt today. It basically had little value for the material realm, and thought it was evil, to such an extent that the Gnostics couldn't believe that Jesus as a Divine being had come in the flesh. Many New Testament letters are directed at correcting this thought. A biblical worldview includes a value for the spiritual and also the material because it's His world, He made it and He said it was good. What I am saying is I had relegated the value of good things that are material good things, like God's material provision, healing, circumstantial favour, promotion at work etc. These things weren't as spiritual or valuable as things like forgiveness, righteousness, going to heaven etc. And because they weren't as spiritual they weren't as valuable, and in some cases they were even suspect.

It seemed that the evangelicalism we, as the Christian community, had inherited was influenced by this kind of thinking, perhaps in an attempt to avoid materialism. Or even a genuine desire to avoid a preoccupation with the gift, not the giver. A sacred-secular divide emerges as we value a system of thought that elevates the spiritual manifestations of the goodness of God above the material ones. David had no such problem. He said *"Bless the Lord, O my soul, and forget not ALL His benefits; he forgives all your sins and heals all your diseases..."* (Psalm 103).

6.3 Bridging Heaven and Earth

<u>Growing dreams</u>

The accumulation of disappointment, if we let it defer our hope, has a shrinking affect on our dreams. What we hope for becomes smaller, until perhaps it's all about what we can do with little or no help from God or others. Most big dreams, God-shaped dreams, require two things:

1) God's resources, His help, because it's beyond you at your biggest stretch.
2) The help of others, a team or friends who understand what you are going after and cheer you on; people who add their talents and strengths to the process to see the dream fulfilled.

If your hope in God drains away and your trust in people dwindles through tough relational issues, the tendency is to pull your horns in and shrink the dream to reduce the need for those who appear to have let you down, which can include God and man.

It's a classic enemy tactic. We are in profound union with the God of the universe who partners with us. A key way He does this is to do more than we can ask or imagine (think) – Ephesians 3:20. If this inner envisioning and dreaming can be damaged, or our imagination stunted, our partnership can be limited. God likes to take a dream and super-size it. If we have stopped dreaming for greater things He has much less to work with.

If you think about it, it makes sense. God is infinite in power and therefore possibilities. He is good and wants earth to look increasingly like heaven, to be increasingly full of Him. That's the best thing for everyone: He is not an egotist, He is the best thing. He is also committed to partnership with man and we are His co-workers.

How does God involve His co-workers, who are limited, in the creation of the impossible in their reality? It's easy for God, but new territory for them. How does the Unlimited One work successfully through the limited ones? What's the bridge? He gave us an imagination: a capacity to dream beyond the confines of the normal, the rational and the currently possible. That is the place where heaven's possibilities can incubate.

Bridging heaven and earth

Think of the power of the imagination. Authors imagine whole worlds and sweep us up into great stories about fantastic places that only exist in their minds. We can now turn them into film with phenomenal special effects that bring these imagined realities to life before our eyes. But they still don't exist in any solid form. They are alternate realities that remain in the realm of imagination.

God-dreams have the power to imagine a heavenly reality and to be the means of them becoming real in the earth. A God-picture, an imagined future that is the fruit of your partnership with Him in your imagination, can become a real future, a solid manifestation of your partnership with heaven.

I have tended to think of dreams as a luxury or even a frivolity; we need to get the work done. I guess my image is of dreamy people who float around not getting stuck in. This is not what is in view here. It's our inner world, illuminated by hope, creating dreams that God works with and expands so that His heavenly reality can come to the earth through us.

The biblical view of the heart is inclusive of the thoughts and imaginations, not just feelings and emotions. In our hearts we think, reflect and meditate. Guarding my heart involves the renewal of mental pathways, unclogging the arteries of the mind so a Holy Spirit-inspired imagination can flourish; the springs of supernatural life can then flow (Proverbs 4:23). This involves resisting the mind-shrinking effects of cynicism and disappointment.

I am not here referring to the growth or depletion of intellect. Caring for our intellectual abilities is important; however, an intellect that is shaped by scepticism can powerfully resist the kind of imagining we are discussing here.

Are my dreams in keeping with who I am and who He is? Do they reflect my true identity? Before I was a Christian I dreamed of owning my own home and having a car and a family, and that was it. Now I dream of stadiums of people experiencing creative miracles, cancers healed, blind eyes opened and mighty churches that experience so much of God in worship that it's hard to stay in your skin. Churches that change the culture and atmosphere of their cities.

Here's a list of common thinking that inhibits hopes and dreams:

1) What I'm thinking of has never been done before
2) I am too young; I am too old
3) I am not smart enough
4) I am too weak
5) I have no money
6) I have no time
7) The last thing I tried didn't work

Most of our reasons revolve around our past experience, our sense of identity and our lack of resources. The more we see Him as a good Father, backing us with His resources, and see ourselves as loved, powerful sons, the more dreams grow. We then see the obstacles bow the knee to the Father/son partnership that is you and God. He knows no limits and is inviting you into His reality. He is fully aware of your reality, but isn't limited by it. Your reality is a thing to Him, it's something he cares about, but never in a way that He submits to its constraints or your feelings about it. He is limitless and wants to release that resource into your world so that it is shaped and expanded by His.

It's vital that we learn to pull down imaginations and everything that sets itself up against the knowledge of Christ. Broken, wrongly focused or limited imagination can hinder the work of Jesus in the earth.

The enduring value of endurance

It would be wrong to close out this chapter without a word about endurance. Not everything is instant. We love the suddenlies and the immediate breakthroughs. We also need to value waiting, testing times and endurance. The process is valuable. Endurance produces character, and character produces hope (Romans 5:4).

A couple of years ago my son Luke and his family stayed with us for a few months. I came downstairs from my office one day to find Zach, who was two at the time, sitting on the bottom step. He was quite still, especially for an energetic two-year-old. I said "Zach, what are you doing?" He said "I'm waiting." I had never heard a two-year-old say that, or do it quite as well as he was. A moment later I saw his mum, Claire, and asked what was going on. She said it was good for little kids to learn to wait; not everything comes when they want it to. She was training him to wait. I forget now what he was waiting for, but it was important to him. He sat there for quite a while, learning to wait until the moment came. Then he was ready and excited.

Every promise from God that produces hope and expectation does get tested. James 1:3 talks about the testing of faith. We see it in Joseph, who had an amazing dream of influence as a teenager, but went through great testing before it was fulfilled.

Delay and testing, when responded to well, actually produce more hope. Endurance creates character that can maturely carry the blessing promised. Continuing to count Him faithful in the face of trial and delay is a major piece of character-building strength for a believer. Patience and endurance produce godly hope. Delay is not "no" from God, it's a preparation for a greater day.

Keep the dream alive.

Endnote

a. Just to note there are many excellent ways to the healing of the heart which are not in the scope of this book. Sozo and other excellent ministries have arisen to bless and heal us, so our hearts work well. This chapter highlights our responsibilities in looking after our hope and our hearts.

FINAL WORD

UNTIL

For biblical background, see Ephesians 4:13; Ephesians 5:25-27; 1 Corinthians 15:25; Hebrews 10:12-13; Acts 2:35; John 14:12; 2 Peter 3:12.

I am an occasional cook. I like doing it, but I need instructions. I cook by numbers, so a good recipe is really important to me. I need quantities, and it's vital I have timings. Theresa, who is a great cook, works by sense, feel and whether "it looks right." She has tons of experience. She is so skilled she can change recipes on the run and it often improves the outcome. I stand in awe!

One of my pet hates is making white sauce, which is a base for quite a lot of things. The reason is you keep it on the heat and keep stirring it until it's the right consistency. It has to thicken, but not too much, and if you don't pay attention it goes lumpy. I also dislike recipe instructions like "heat the onions over a medium heat until they caramelise." I like a time. Tell me that in five minutes it is done; all this "stir until it's a smooth consistency" is frustrating to me. You can't leave it, you have to give it focus.

"Until" is a time word, but it doesn't tell you how long in minutes or years. You can't set your timer and walk away; you have to pay attention to see that the conditions are met. "Until" is precise in a different way. White sauce is definitely ready when it's ready, you just have stir and keep an eye on it until it is. In cooking, "until" asks for continued involvement. Some outcomes, like smooth sauce, are not automatic without the cook's continued input until it is what it's supposed to be.

We are living in "until." The end will come when the sauce is thickened. The return of Jesus is contingent on some things being ready. He is at the Father's right hand until all His enemies have been made His footstool. Jesus is seated at the right hand of the Father, but He has yet to put His feet up! This isn't saying the enemy isn't fundamentally defeated; that happened at the cross. It's saying His victory needs to be implemented and enforced. Stir the sauce and get rid of the lumps – we have a responsibility to partner with the Lord to remove hinderances!

It is true that gifts will cease, that ministries will become redundant, because they are given for a time, but it's an "until" - until we all reach the full measure of the stature of Christ. There is a measure of maturity for the Church that means she is full of Christ, displaying Him to the world around. Equipping the saints only ends when they are equipped and the Church is standing in the full measure of the stature of Jesus. We have to give the process focused attention to get the outcome the Lord has described.

If you could sum up the goal of this book, it would be to stimulate biblical hope for the emergence of a Body of Christ that is of the stature and fullness of Christ in the earth. We do so by challenging some preconceived approaches; digging into the divide between knowledge and experience and bringing those two essential realities back together as one; telling a story that is being repeated around the world; and promoting a vision of culture that looks more like heaven than the earth that too easily bleeds into our thinking.

This is not hope for a rescue of the Church, but hope for

a wedding; a beautiful glorious bride that has made herself ready for her King to come. Where the Spirit and the Bride together say "Come, Lord." I am believing for a church that enjoys and releases to the world everything Jesus already won for us. That makes it possible for the world to believe in His resurrection and victory because we display it.

The fullness of Christ we are to display is exactly that, everything we know of Him displayed through us into the world – His power; His wisdom; His character. We can't allow ourselves opt-outs or some clever compartmentalising of the attributes of Jesus that says the display of some aspects of His nature belong in a distant future. It's now the world needs to see Him; it's now that a full and holistic display of the resurrected Jesus is to be seen in the world.

At times it has looked like the church has limited the Jesus she was seeking to embody to His character and His message. The Church believed that was enough; that was our offer to the world. However, we are not fully displaying Him until we also display all the supernatural attributes He demonstrated along with the "more" He promised we could do. We are not displaying Him fully until we reflect the atmosphere of Heaven in the way we function.

Let the flame of hope for this be fanned into a fire in your heart, so you too will hope, and so pursue this dream. Dream a dream that grips you so strongly that the many obstacles and setbacks will not quench the relentless nature of the hope burning in your heart.

Impossible dream, perhaps. But all things are possible for him who believes.

For more information about
Hope School of Supernatural Life

contact HSSL@hopechurchglasgow.org

For more information about Hope Church Glasgow,
it's equipping conferences and resources

contact admin@hopechurchglasgow.org

www.ingramcontent.com/pod-product-compliance
Lightning Source LLC
LaVergne TN
LVHW051558070426
835507LV00021B/2651